3~~~

The Power of
Equilibrium

A Plan for Self-Discovery and Unparalleled Balance
For Your Best Life Now

Gary Westfal
Kirk Hendricks
Colleen Riddle

3Thirty3, LLC
In Association with
G-Life Enterprises Corp.

ISBN: 978-0-9992220-9-6
Library of Congress Control Number: 2017955792

BOOK DESIGN BY: 3Thirty3, LLC,
in association with G-Life Enterprises Corp.

Gary Westfal, Author, Concept Art
Kirk Hendricks, Author, Concept Art
Colleen Riddle, Author, Concept Art
Scott Grinnell, Graphic Artist

All images are the original creation of 3Thirty3, LLC and G-Life
Enterprises Corporation and/or permissions have been secured and/or
released for use by their originator or rightful owner and documentation
is on file with the publisher.

Printed in the United States of America

This book is dedicated to
those who are ready to wake up to a life of
amazing possibilities.

To: Diane

May this book inspire
you and help you find
balance in your life!

♡

2020

ACKNOWLEDGMENTS

It has long been said that there is power in numbers. There is an even *greater* power in yielding to those things that give us pause while we consider the quiet leading of wisdom, insight, and knowledge. It is with this quiet leading and the inspiration of a common-core mindset that we deliver the content of our message.

We began our journey, not unlike most, with an idea that spoke to all three of us. This idea first came to us by way of inspiration—that quiet, yet powerful force that if duly recognized and seized upon, will forever change the course of a life. What at first appeared to be coincidence later turned out to be the answer to a call for direction and leading we all seem to be searching for. We had no way of knowing that answer would beautifully coalesce the lives of three totally different people with a common goal to deliver an inspiring message of personal transformation to the masses.

What if, we wondered…*what if* we could merge our individual strengths, talents, and life experiences while using the power of our collective passions to help people realize their true potential? What would it look like? Where would we begin?

The process of creating this book and the powerful content it contains emanates from a passion we each have to help people. It is our sincere desire to share the insight and information we have discovered that has led each of us to a greater sense of purpose through our own personal transformations. Knowing our purpose has fostered the goodness of life we all seek in terms of physical, emotional, and spiritual balance, leading to the ultimate purpose of life: Happiness! The discovery of *our* purpose has led us to so many amazing breakthroughs in life and has ultimately led us to *you*.

Each co-author of this book brings a unique perspective and set of life skills that strikes at the core of truth as it relates to what works when seeking a meaningful life's purpose. The insight, awareness, methods, and inspiration we bring throughout the pages of this book serve as a platform to launch your own personal development plan—your own *transformation*—leading to your ideal life…your *best* life.

Writing a book can be an arduous undertaking, requiring concentration, dedication, and focus on the goal of producing valuable, relevant, and inspiring content. There are so many details to watch, manage, and care for just to stay on the right path to publication. If not for the love, support, dedication, and management of our *entire* team, we would not have been able to publish this book. To everyone on the team—our spouses, our families, our artists, mentors, advisors, contributors, and editors—we thank you, we love you, and we are forever humbly grateful.

TABLE OF CONTENTS

INTRODUCTION

333

This book is *not* about numbers. It is about *balance*. It is not about numerology but about *human-ology*—that is, the science and understanding of human nature as seen and described in the three overarching aspects of humankind: *body, mind,* and *spirit.* Each individual aspect by itself presents a powerful force in the unique makeup of our nature. When considered collectively, however, they present an entirety of the *whole-person* concept, the likes of which each aspect compliments and compounds upon the effect of the other. Despite the numerical disclaimer, however, there is ample reason to consider the role and peculiarity of numbers as they apply to their places in the balance of life.

Throughout our research, we noticed the number 3 continued to make an uncanny reappearance from almost every conceivable angle—from the inception of our inspiration to the formation of our team and the construct and content of the message. The fact that the number 3 provides a foundational framework for the three aspects of the human makeup elicits a curious consideration, and hence, a sincere attempt to offer a plausible explanation of the role of numbers on the bearing of balance when considering those three aspects of our human nature.

The number 3 symbolizes the principle of growth and signifies the presence of a synergy the likes of which form the essence of who we are and what we are capable of from a physical, psychological, and spiritual perspective. The number 3 also represents the principles of increase, expansion, maturity, and abundance on the physical, emotional, financial, and spiritual levels.

We think of the number 3 as representing an equilateral triangle, each side and point being equal and distributed evenly within and among a well-formed triad. Three is the numerical representation of truth—irrespective of right or wrong—pure and simple. It is with this simple philosophy, and our sincere desire to bring the truth in the form of our collective insight, which has additive value across the three spectra that connects us all—*body, mind,* and *spirit.*

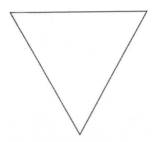

The equilateral triangle above represents a diametrically opposed perspective from what is typically seen as an "upright" representation of the triangle. It is from this unorthodox perspective that we gain insight into the nature of a *reflective* self. The reflective nature also symbolizes the union of the opposing principles of *ac-*

tive and *passive, error* and *truth, ignorance* and *wisdom, yin* and *yang,* and *good* and *evil* that exists throughout life, as we know it. This perspective reminds us of everything that waits to be discovered beyond the comfort and familiarity of what we currently know and believe to be true. In other words, there is so much more to learn if we will only pause and take notice.

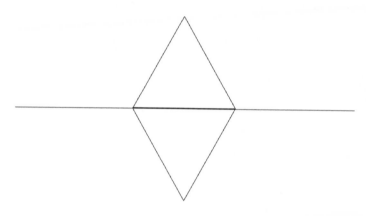

Harmony and balance are absolute essential states if we are to realize our true potential. In order to reach these optimal states we must possess the knowledge and wisdom it takes to understand and achieve them. *333* delivers insightful information through practical and inspirational narratives that are designed to bring clarity, power, and change to the forefront of our lives through the individual and collective lenses of the authors—each an authority in their field of focus and wise in the application of the principles of achievement and personal enrichment. Theirs is a message that will enable you to see things from a position of power that serves to remind us all that we can have, be, do, and experience *everything* life has to offer.

The power of 3 can be seen throughout life if we pause long enough to recognize its significance. This number is known to have influence far beyond its seemingly insignificant expression of value. In fact, it is among the first values we are exposed to as children as we learn to count; it drives art, science, and religion; it is symmetrical, spiritual, and orderly. For example, are you aware that the Earth is the third planet from the sun, or that DNA is one of three major macromolecules necessary for life?

In religion we see three parts of the holy trinity—three people crucified at Christ's death before he was raised from the dead… on the third day. Buddhists take refuge in the Three Jewels or Treasures, and there are three parts to the Hindu Trimurti. Three is indeed a cornerstone in the concept of humankind's perception of beauty, form, function, and universal significance. There are three distinct components to the Yin and Yang of Taoism whereby "One gives rise to two, two gives rise to three, and three gives rise to everything." *Three* being the interaction between Yin and Yang. Three also represents the past, present, and future—a concept we use to delineate our existence in a rather futile attempt to measure and define our lives through the passage of time. And it is by no means incidental that 333 is a book written by three authors in three sections with three chapters each.

333 is a book about balance, awareness, and introspect. It is a book that provides a distinct advantage of three unique perspectives of the three primary, overarching aspects of life. It is a book that can bring about the changes you seek to transform your life from *what is* to the limitless possibilities that are yours to define and freely imagine.

333 is a book about…*you*—a powerful three-letter word that captures the essence of everything.

SECTION ONE

Body

by
Colleen Riddle

CHAPTER 1

Your Amazing Body

How Action Produces Results Every Time

You have an amazing body!

Do you realize your body is comprised of approximately 37 trillion cells? In fact, your heart beats at a rate of about 100,000 times per day, pumping 5.5 liters of blood per minute. Your amazing eyes can distinguish between 2.3 and 7.5 million different colors. Your brain is 73 percent water, which makes even a modest amount of dehydration a factor you should monitor carefully. Even a mere 2 percent dehydration begins to negatively affect attention, memory, and cognitive skills. Of course, most of us know the importance of muscle function. Without muscle we would essentially be immobile and unable to accomplish even the most basic, life-sustaining motor skills.

If it were not for our amazing body's ability to self-regulate and maintain itself, we would be overwhelmed with monitoring, adjusting, and maintaining the essential functions of life…just to live. Fortunately, our responsibility is relegated to a few tasks and behaviors that allow us to decide how efficiently these systems operate. Of course, these tasks (physical exercise and a wellness regimen) alone are of relative importance to how we feel, how we look, and how long we are apt to live. How important are these behaviors? Well, ignore them at your own peril. How's that for a reality check?

So, what is it about physical exercise that we so casually dismiss on a regular basis, yet end up feeling absolutely transformed once we push ourselves through it? There is a reason we begin this book on a discussion about health. Everything emanates from our health, from the health of our mind to the healthy awareness of our spirit. Everything else is secondary. The balance of our bank account is irrelevant. Our social status is unimportant. *None* of it will prevent disease, sickness, or illnesses that rob the quality of life of an otherwise healthy state of being.

There are few "sure things" in life that will provide a comparative return on your investment than a healthy lifestyle. Think about the last time you invested your hard-earned money into something—real estate, the stock market, your 401K. Those may have easily been met by disappointment, or at least a bit of uncertainty, as you watched the fluctuations in value occur. An investment in a healthy lifestyle is one of the most *certain* investments you can make. The return on investment is far and away the absolute best in terms of what you can do with the results.

> *"Man spends his life making money*
> *only to spend his money saving his life."*
> ~ Chinese Proverb

Life is precious. You may not fully appreciate that statement, depending on your age. But the aging process will catch up with you sooner or later. And if you haven't fully prepared for it, you will "suddenly" find yourself out of shape and unprepared to

live life to its fullest. Some of you reading this can attest to how quickly health, fitness, and vitality can erode.

One Day is...Now

"I don't have *time* to exercise or eat right." Sound familiar? I talk to people all the time who tell me how they have the best intentions but cannot seem to find a way to place a simple fitness routine into their lives. The fact that they see their health as something that resides *outside* of them and that they must *fit* it into their lives speaks to the central issue. A simple mindset shift is typically all that is in order here. After all, it is possible to reverse our aversion toward the physical discomfort and inconvenience of exercise and generate desire to fuel the process of a healthy lifestyle.

There are those who proclaim that their intention is to be in better shape "someday." Well, last time I checked, "someday" is not among the days of the week on the calendar. A fresh mindset allows us to boldly declare a *specific* time in which we will take action to change the course and quality of our lives. For instance, "now" would be a very good time to start.

Results or Excuses—You Can't Have Both

As a fitness professional, I have a front row seat to the very interesting tug-of-war games our minds like to play when it comes to actually doing the things it takes to be healthy. On one side there is a sincere desire for health. On the other side are all the reasons and excuses we tend to use—let's call it *life*. Life represents the *external* forces and circumstances that influence our

internal resolve to be healthy. Our struggle with life's demands is nothing new. Yet, when it comes to taking actions that support a healthy lifestyle, we find it easy to procrastinate or avoid altogether. If we find it so easy to give in to these convincing forces, why isn't it just as easy to overcome them? Because...

What is easy to do is also easy not to do.

To affect real and lasting physical change, the first thing we need to work on is the brain. Our brain controls all of our bodily functions. As we discovered earlier, most of these functions are inherently automatic, from the timing of our heartbeat to the sensitivities of our eyesight and sense of smell. The rest is up to us.

Conditioning our mind to perform even the most basic maintenance functions for the benefit of our physical health can be a challenge, to say the least. Why is that? Well, for starters, physical fitness maintenance requires work. Our mind is conditioned to equate work with pain. We humans are motivated by two diametrically-opposed fundamental forces—pleasure and pain.

Despite knowing long-term results of physical exertion (work) are associated with better overall health, we hesitate when we are first presented with pain! It is for this reason we should begin with training the *brain* in order to associate physical exercise with the long-term effect of optimal health, which is overall a more satisfying and pleasurable experience.

One of the most difficult things to do is to start something new, especially when that *something* is most closely associated with a painful experience. This is precisely where the importance of mind training comes in handy. Your mind will resist pain unless you force your physical actions to power through an experience in order to "prove" to your mind the *advantage* of this type of pain. This phase is called the *determination* phase.

Determination Fueled by Emotion

Determination is fueled by perseverance towards a difficult goal or objective despite the obstacles. Determination is a behavioral trait that drives us to continue trying to do or achieve something of difficulty. It is the fuel that allows us to act in spite a painful or unpleasant experience. Practiced consistently, determination typically yields favorable results. As these results are achieved, *motivation* develops. As motivation develops, our determination increases to a point where our brain is conditioned to accept and associate the experience as a positive one, even in the presence of pain.

Motivation allows us to gain an increasing level of psychological control over the conditions we must overcome to reach our objective. The closer we get to our objective, the more our brain learns to associate pain with the *temporary* nature of obstacles we face as we map out and pursue our goals. Our brain, therefore, learns that it can overcome pain through determination. This is the essence of motivation—*knowing* we can overcome obstacles to achieve our goals and desired objectives. In essence, we are capable of reprogramming our mind's *perception* of certain physical sensations from a negative to a positive experience.

Our motivation is directly connected to the reasons *why* we do or do not take action. Oftentimes, the reasons why we refrain from taking action are simply more compelling than why we *should* take action. We say things like, "I'll get to it after the game is over," or "I don't have time today." These are indicators that should serve as a warning sign of complacency that never turn out to be good for us in the long run.

What is *your* motivation? What are the obstacles that keep getting in the way of your momentum? Each and every one of us has something that drives us to take action. Motivation is an ally that will faithfully serve us beyond measure if we will just acknowledge, embrace, and exploit it.

The story I often hear is how some people have no motivation whatsoever. They avoid a healthy routine because of the associated pain their mind has convinced them is connected to a healthy lifestyle. They interpret *exercise* as "work" and *healthy eating choices* as a "diet." These perceptions convince them to avoid any activity that will actually enhance their overall health and well-being. Some use the demands of life as an excuse to avoid a healthy lifestyle by placing the importance of their own health in subordination to "higher life priorities." The sad reality is that there should, in fact, be *no* higher priority.

I have been successful in helping people identify their *why*—the central compelling reason they act or behave the way they do. I work with people to effectively overpower the negative associations they have with a healthy lifestyle. If this sounds like something you may need some assistance with, I urge you not to give up, no matter your age, fitness level, or circumstances. There is *always* someone available to help you through this phase of achievement.

Your ability to use determination to find your way to motivation will pay huge dividends. As motivation takes shape, we are better able to tap into the power of our determination to push through areas and times of difficulty. Each new milestone we achieve feeds our motivation and strengthens our resolve to accomplish our goals. There is a positive feedback system waiting within each of us to be utilized, and once we allow it to begin, the process will continue with relatively little maintenance. Think of this as the "breath" of our intent.

Amazing things begin to unfold as we turn away from what we know are poor choices. With each new achievement, we see motivation smiling upon us as we gradually begin to see a trans-formation taking place from within that is virtually unstoppable. In fact, the only thing that *can* stop you is...*you*. This is the pre-cise moment when excuses fade and a positive transformation begins to manifest.

I'm reminded of a story of how my husband found *his* mo-tivation that helped him power through to his goal of "achieving less"—less weight that is. You see, he discovered his motivation in the form of pain—the pain of his belt. As he bent over to tie his shoes one day, his belt pinched his stomach. Ouch! I had been (somewhat) gently encouraging him to make some changes in his physical life for some time. After all, he lives with *me*—a personal fitness trainer...*hello!* But I realized all too well, even then, that until *he* was ready—no matter what I said or what my professional credentials—nothing would change. I am happy to report that he ultimately discovered something he enjoys that provides him with a level of physical activity that helps him live a healthier lifestyle—cycling. He has been pedaling ever since. And the best part is his belt no longer reminds him of the need to change his lifestyle.

The scenario above is one in which a physical reminder of pain eventually became stronger than the desire to embrace an otherwise ordinary life devoid of physical fitness activity. The truth is, his age was catching up with him and was evidenced by an increasing waistline. It was enough to spike his determina-tion to take action and be consistent enough to begin seeing real results.

Over the course of my career as a fitness trainer I have dis-covered many ways to help people see the value of a sound fitness regimen leading to a life of wellness. I have successfully helped hundreds of people overcome external circumstances and in-ternal (self-imposed) limitations that get in the way of creating healthy habits. Most people are surprised when they discover the simplicity of the formula to a healthy lifestyle. Look, this doesn't have to be complicated. In fact, I have always found simplicity to be the best approach in terms of instilling consistency and follow-through—two of the most essential elements of success in any form.

Consider the following three steps to help you find the motivation you may need to reprioritize your life and permit you to bring about a balanced healthy change. I call these steps *Lights, Camera, Action!* I can assure you that these changes will bring a lot more to you than physical health. You will be more confident, think clearer, and be happier as you begin living a revitalized life, or, as I prefer to call it—living *full out!*

Lights...

Something magical happens when we turn on the lights. Quite simply, we can see! In order to launch a successful plan, we must be able to *see*, or clearly identify, what we are up against.

The first step in getting the proverbial scales of life to balance is to identify our *why*. This is one of the most important aspects in finding equilibrium, so put some thought here. Don't just say, "I want to lose weight," or "I want to get healthier." Discover *why* you want to lose weight. *Why* do you want to get healthy? *Why* do you want to *stay* healthy? Is your motivation driven by love, fear, or anger? It's okay to tap into those emotions until you can transition to a mindset more conducive to sustaining the healthiest image of you. Without a compelling reason *why*, we remain disconnected, and our efforts are subject to the risk of failure and frustration.

Examination of our why allows us to see the essence of our true self in virtually every aspect. What do you see when you examine *your* why? You most likely see the difference in where you are versus where you desire to be. That's a great starting point. The more intimate you become with your why, the better able you are to transition to an "end-state" image of who you desire to become, which is the healthiest outlook to have.

There are as many reasons to get healthy as there are to do nothing at all. The choice is ultimately yours to make, but until you identify the reason—your why—you are likely to do little, if anything at all. So, what do you say? Can you find your why? If not, turn on the lights, so you may see more clearly. Once you do you will be ready to take the next step.

Camera…

Perspective is everything. Who among us has taken a picture and not been absolutely *compelled* to see it right away. Why do we do that? Well, some of us want to make sure we actually look good. One way we do that is by looking at ourselves from the alternate perspective of the camera lens—a photograph.

To perform the second step in finding balance we need to examine ourselves from a selfless point of view. This step calls upon you to find a quiet place to contemplate without distractions.

Separate your spiritual and psychological self from the physical and see yourself from an alternate perspective. As you do this I want you to mentally turn down the sounds and focus mostly on what you see and how you feel. Are you smiling? If so, can you identify what is making you smile? What is your emotional state of mind? Is there anything you discern that is keeping you from becoming more active? Notice the emotional changes as you enter this state. This state of awareness does not have to be temporary, and it does not have to remain out of reach. It can be yours at any time you wish. This psychological exercise is a lot like physical exercise—the more you practice, the better you are able to perform. The insight and introspection you gain can make all the difference in terms of what you see as a solution, to the things you can change to enhance your fitness level.

Contrary to popular belief, your health does *not* have to be tied to a gym membership or some other form of organized sports. In fact, you will get more out of your fitness routine and stay with it longer if you are having *fun*. A gym—although a great place to get into shape and stay healthy—is not for everybody. So don't allow it be your excuse *not* to get into the shape you desire and deserve. After all, you're looking for results—not a gym membership you will never use. Once you discover an activity that brings you happiness (and results), you will have a compelling reason that will drive you to the third step…

Action!

Now that you have identified your why, and you have a clearer perspective of yourself, you are ready for the third step—Action! This third step, quite simply, is *doing it*. Sounds simple enough. But, unfortunately, this is where most people fall short. Why? The answer is best explained in the following example:

You have made a decision to use running as your activity to get in shape. You are excited to get going, but you realize you need the right gear, so you purchase all of the latest running gear—the best shoes, matching shorts, etc.

The first day, you wake up early and set off on your new running regimen. You are on top of the world as you feel the wind in your hair and smell the fresh air surge through your nose. You find yourself wondering why you waited *so* long to do something like this to get into shape. "This is easy," you declare.

The following day comes around and you suddenly find that you can't move! Muscle soreness has set in and is not shy about reminding you of the consequences of your choice to get into better shape. In fact, you cannot even get out of bed without assistance.

Doubt begins to set in as your mind takes over and tries to rationalize how anyone in their right mind would intentionally desire to hurt like this *every day*. Your pleasurable running experience is rudely interrupted by the pain of muscle soreness. So you tap into your power of determination and grudgingly convince yourself to give it *one more try*.

You are astonished to discover that the very same soreness continues even after a second run, so you seek the advice from a friend (a non-runner). That friend tells you, in no uncertain terms, "I told you so," and you go back to your old habits of no muscle pain, where you are most familiar, and end up selling all of that excellent running gear on eBay. Does this sound familiar? If so, I encourage you to regroup and *do it* again. (Notice I didn't say, "try.")

"Do or do not. There is no try."
~ Yoda

People often tell me they have taken these action steps in the past only to fall into the trap I describe above. And my first questions are, "How long did it take you to get into the shape you are in? Did it happen overnight or did you spend years taking your health for granted?" Usually I get a confused look until my point makes sense.

Most people spend years making one poor decision after another and then expect to reverse the process in a matter of days. Any one of these poor choices by themselves is insignificant, but compounded by time and frequency, leads to the current state of dismal, unhealthy, and unhappy affairs. A great book called *The Slight Edge* by Jeff Olson, discusses the compounding effects of time and frequency on our seemingly small (but collective) decisions. We all make choices every day—some good and some not so good. And many times the decisions we are faced with are just as easy to execute—or avoid altogether. In the context of health and exercise, skipping a workout is no big deal...or is it? Skipping just *one* exercise session is typically inconsequential to our *physical* fitness level but can be devastating to our *psychological* balance, having a huge impact on our ability to maintain the consistency required for results.

We live in a time of immediate gratification and the mindset of, "If I can't have it now, I don't want or need it." People have spent billions of dollars on the quick fix, only to be left with a closet full of late night infomercial products promising quick results with hardly any work. Are you beginning to see the insanity? We have been programmed to expect immediate results, so we get frustrated when the results do not appear right away.

It is important to set ourselves up for success right from the start, because the action step is where we are most vulnerable. It is that critical first step where excuses are lurking and many a good plan fails to materialize. Why is that? For starters, most people try to change everything at once. You are excited, so you drastically change your diet and your habits as you boldly take on a huge, new fitness routine. Your enthusiasm and radical behavioral shift is a massive shock to your body that brings about pain. Physical pain is something that causes your mind to create ways to avoid a repeat experience and is a destroyer of good intentions.

You must keep in mind that your current habits and rituals have been at work for years. An attempt to change everything in one fell swoop rarely works out well. You need an action plan that *collaborates* with your body and is your ally, not your enemy. A plan that is built on success principles starts with *small* changes and consistent action that, in the end, leads to *big* results.

Small Changes Lead to Big Results

One of my clients—we'll call her Michelle—was overweight and frustrated. Michelle came to me looking for a way to begin to change the direction of her lifestyle and lose the weight she had been carrying around for over twenty years. Of all the methods I employ to help people physically, the one most important aspect of my success formula is to understand a person's primary motivation for seeking a physical transformation. As I set out to help Michelle discover her *why*, I found that she and her husband desperately wanted to have a baby. Her doctor told her she was too heavy and needed to lose weight in order to facilitate a safe pregnancy. What her doctor was *really* telling her is that she was not healthy enough to bear a child. She was in tears as she painfully explained her longing to be a mother, and she came to the realization that, in order to do that, she had to be healthier.

I created a plan with her and we began an exercise program she could grow into and adapt to her lifestyle. I asked her to create two goals to focus on each week (we affectionately called them "baby steps"). I asked her to choose one goal relating to nutrition and one goal pertaining to exercise.

19

She shared with me how drinking soda was her greatest weakness. She admitted to drinking three to five sodas *a day!* So instead of going "cold turkey" with the soda, I asked her to set a weekly goal of no more than two sodas a day for a week. She was apprehensive, but the power of her *why* compelled her to take on the challenge.

Two weeks later, she reported that our plan was working! Not only did it help her realize her soda consumption was a ritual born more out of habit than desire, but, by substituting water and other healthy alternatives, she really did not miss the soda at all. In fact, she actually began feeling better. The changes she made, coupled with her sense of accomplishment, provided just the boost she needed to launch an entirely new life chapter in the pursuit of her goals. Do you see the power of this positive feedback system yet? As a result, she began to believe in herself, which is one of the most important aspects of the journey, and gained a new appreciation for health and a true sense of well-being. Michelle continued her new rituals of healthy living, lost over twenty pounds, and, I'm happy to report, she and her husband are the proud parents of a baby boy.

We can learn quite a bit from stories like Michelle's. They provide inspiring examples of how this philosophy can be applied to virtually *all* areas of our lives. It has been said that it takes, on average, twenty-one days to create a new habit. Your new habits will be formed by applying *small* changes to your daily rituals. Attaining and maintaining a level of good health is *not* a quick fix, nor is it a destination. It is a *lifestyle* based on consistent, smart choices. Remember, Rome was not built in a day, but by placing one stone (one small change) into place at a time, it became a monument that stood the test of time.

Want to know one of the best "secrets" to good health? I mentioned it once already: *Consistency.* It's not how you *start*, but how you *finish* that matters. Consider the running example again. My advice is to start slow, maybe walking and running for a mile (or around the block if that is all you can do at first). Then, gradually increase the intensity of your activity. Do a little more tomorrow than you do today, but do something *every* day.

Those who are new to fitness are simply unaware of the physiological and mental changes our body goes through as we adjust to a new training regimen or routine. It is not unlike most other areas of our lives where something new can sometimes be a painful experience at first. But rest assured, the pain is not only alleviated over time, it can also become a source of inspiration and invigoration. As you learn to manipulate the very pain you despise, you are better able to control the health and shape of your most precious *physical* asset—your body. Remember, this doesn't have to be complicated, and can actually be rather enjoyable once you get the hang of it.

CHAPTER 2

Diet

A Four-Letter Word You Should Eliminate

When it comes to your health, nutrition is the number one contributor to your body composition and to the overall functionality of the vital systems that keep you alive. In fact, nutrition accounts for approximately 70 percent of your state of health. It cannot be overlooked and is an absolute essential aspect to your overall health. That said, you have likely come to understand the importance of exercise just by reading the first chapter of this book. It's a must.

Physical activity combined with proper nutrition helps to promote strong bones, muscle, and the efficient performance of vital organs. It all starts and ends with what you put into your mouth. Look, we can train or exercise together five times a week, have the best workout sessions in the best conditions, but if you're consuming empty calories or junk food, your results will be…empty. This is simply a common sense approach to the physical fitness struggles I see time and time again.

The struggle for a balanced state of health stems from a disconnect that occurs when we make simple choices. We *say* we want one thing, but our actions tell a different story. A good visual for this on-going battle is the proverbial angel on one shoulder and devil on the other, both whispering words of influential wisdom into our ears. On one side there is health, and on the other is sickness and an early grave. Now, it seems as if, when faced with these two choices, the decision would be easy. However, we don't often take the sickness and early grave option all that seriously. Why is that? One reason is the relatively slow evidence of a declining state of health.

The dilemma of making the right choice is not so easy to overcome because we are typically distracted by this thing called life, along with the *conditioned* aspects of pleasure and pain we associate with it. The demands of life tend to take an arrogant priority until life suddenly succumbs to the low priority we place on keeping ourselves in a reasonably good state of health. However, we must all understand that the energy we are consuming is literally going to be what we will physically become. *What* do you want to be?

Two of the most powerful aspects of choice are not on our side from the outset. Knowing these aspects from the start gives us an inside advantage on overcoming choices that are not in our best physical interest.

Lies and Misconceptions

The first powerful aspect of choice is the lies we tell ourselves. Lies such as, "If I had more time I'd exercise." Or, "I'm too old to start changing my lifestyle now." Or even, "I can do it tomorrow." Why do we insist on listening to those deceptions? Where do they come from anyway? How can we begin to recognize the lies, and what can we do about it? All great questions…

We typically conjure stories in our head about *nothing* all the time. Think about it (no pun intended)…as your mind drifts to far-away places, how many times have you "made up" a story about something that never has nor ever *will* happen? I'll try to reserve the analysis for my colleague in the section of this book that focuses more on the mind. Suffice it to say, however, that you've experienced this fantasy world of your own on more than one occasion. The reason we tend to listen to these lies is quite simple actually. We humans enjoy a good story. Now, there's nothing wrong with a good story…until it becomes a lie you buy into that changes, or negatively affects or alters, your behavior.

I'm quite certain you have no issues recognizing the stories that present themselves as lies. The lies are patient. They are very good at waiting for their chance to derail you. They tell you things like "the doughnut is your *reward* for being good," or "I've burned a lot of calories this week, so it's okay to drink a soda." We can be masters at justifying our actions and, all too often, play right into the hand of these convincing lies as we develop misconceptions of our own reality—until reality strikes in the form of poor health and sickness.

Recall our mind's association with the pleasure and pain of certain physical activity. We have the capability to control our understanding of the energy we consume in the same manner. Consider how much pleasure there is *after* eating a donut or drinking a soda. None. The pleasure is gone, and if you are mind-fully aware of your body, you will see there is actually pain. Yes, empty calories cause discomfort.

Recognizing the lies often comes *after* you have taken some kind of action that reveals a poor choice. With practice however, you can begin to take control and preempt the lie with your own good judgment.

The grocery store is a great place to witness the conversion of our stories into the lies we tell ourselves. If you glance at the shopping cart of any random shopper, it doesn't take long to determine the general health of the person pushing the cart based on the food selections that are piling up. Consider the following story about the struggle of what we say we *want* versus the actions we typically take.

I was in the grocery store when I saw a client I had trained earlier that morning. As we made eye contact, a look of panic overcame her. She was like a deer in the headlights, frozen. Why? Perhaps it was her fear of confrontation over the revelation of her dietary choices. For a brief time, my presence previously unknown to her, it was obvious she had been influenced more by her desire for what she *perceived* as pleasurable food choices rather than healthier alternatives. She was consumed by a self-perpetuating lie.

Doing my best not to make her feel bad, I smiled and casually joked about the contents of her shopping cart. I was so glad she was brave enough not to turn and run when she saw me, because we were able to use it as a teaching moment. By the way, I could see the shift in her ability to see the truth a few weeks later.

> *"The definition of insanity is to repeatedly do the same thing and expect different results."*
> ~ Albert Einstein

Einstein's quote offers us insight and a great deal of hope, because it gives us the answer to many of life's challenges. Change your habits and you change your world.

A great way to approach this philosophy is to think like someone else. Yes, *someone else*. What I'm actually referring to is *your future self*—that person inside of you; the one that resides in your mind when the world is quiet and no one is looking... the one you see in the mirror...the one that no one else sees. I'd like you to consider making new decisions based on *that* person. By thinking with the end in mind, you automatically begin to change your way of looking at the world as it is and begin making choices that realign you to a new life, as you'd like it to become. The fact is, your future *you* is already present. With clarity, born from presence of mind, you can find the future you whenever you decide.

Body-Mind Connection to a Lifestyle Mindset

Let's take a moment to cast a vision of your future self and center that vision on the aspect of your health. Imagine you are at your ideal weight and fitness level. You are healthy, full of energy, and you are enjoying life to its fullest. Free your mind to envision the absolute *best* life has to offer in this ideal state of health. As you are out for a brisk walk, you catch your reflection in a storefront window. Pause for a moment to enjoy what you see. Smile as you admire a newfound confidence surrounded by a bright new aura. Now step away and continue your walk. Notice how there is a new pep in your step, your shoulders are pulled back, and you're standing tall and confident. You're ready to take on the challenges of life and win! You are driven, living each day as if it is fueled by a purpose...*your* purpose. Redirect your desire toward the pleasure of that mental image, and the image will become your reality.

Think about how *this* new image of you influences the way you handle your health choices. How will the change affect your choice about the doughnut mentioned earlier? Suddenly, your best self emerges with a confident, "No thanks!" Can you see the stark differences?

Have you noticed we have yet to even mention the word *diet*? That's because, for me, "diet" is a four-letter word. Diet has a negative and temporary connotation. How many of us have gone on a diet only to find the pounds we lose come back with a vengeance when we stop dieting? In fact, in many cases, some even seem to find a way to add a few *extra* pounds along the way back to our former, pre-diet self.

What we are talking about here is a *lifestyle shift* leading to a fresh new mindset. A *lifestyle mindset* helps you to create a story of harmony and balance when it comes to food; the *new* story is of self-empowerment and knowledge, two of my favorite things when it comes to health and fitness.

"With profound education comes profound change."

Self-Empowerment

Change is fostered by education and experience. *Profound* change is fostered by the wisdom and insight we gain through rich sources of profound education and experience. These sources help us gain power when we are *empowered* by something or someone that enlightens us to overcome a personal struggle. Empowerment is an *external* source of strength that feeds an *internal* process, allowing us to develop a sense of interconnectedness with the energy we consume and the energy we exert.

Empowerment is characterized by our increasing ability to move away from a deficit-oriented mindset to one that is self-assured, confident, and driven. Think about the frustrations you have experienced in an area of your life. Chances are you were encumbered by your frustration until you discovered a source that provided insight to a solution or resolution.

Your newfound insight produces a breakthrough the likes of which can be life changing. You'll easily recognize a breakthrough as a liberating experience that catapults your life forward. Of all the breakthroughs I have experienced, one of the most significant is when I learned how to reframe the way I view nutrition as a consistent lifestyle choice versus the temporary (and cumbersome) nature of a diet.

Knowledge

Insight and clarity come when we accept information and influences that open the doors to learning. Our willingness to learn new information leads to better understanding, insight, awareness, and clarity of purpose. The more clarity we have, the more we become empowered by the increasing awareness we gain of our innermost self. This newfound awareness leads to wisdom, which is the highest form of learning leading to empowerment. What we are talking about here is exercising the brain in the same way we exercise the muscles. Both are foundations of your balanced physical self and, as you will come to find, your mental and spiritual self as well.

There are plenty of great books and other rich sources covering virtually every aspect of proper nutrition. Find one (or several) that resonates with you. Educate yourself on the fundamental aspects that empower you to make better health-related choices and you will see a transformation take place before your very eyes.

It has long been said that *knowledge is power*. And while this is an accurate statement, the *power* of knowledge is not enough to get you healthy. You must apply wisdom too. I think it's fair to say that most of us realize that a thirsty mind can always be quenched. The more time we spend educating ourselves, the more informed we become. The more informed we are, the more likely we are to make educated decisions. Educated decisions form the foundation for the *actions* we must take to produce healthy change in any area of our life. But, in the end, it is action that we must take if we expect to see change occur.

The pursuit of knowledge produces an exponential return. Of course it's not enough to acquire knowledge for the sake of possessing it. You must also *apply* what you learn. It is by design that I stress action as much I am, because knowledge without action or application is pointless. This concept of learning with a health and fitness lifestyle focus gives a whole new meaning to a "body of knowledge" you now possess. Use it wisely and be empowered to make the changes you desire!

CHAPTER 3

Falling In Love

Falling in Love with the Process

Take a look in the mirror. What do you see, *who* do you see, and *how* do you see it? While these may seem to be rhetorical questions, the premise invites an interesting twist on the process of fitness as it relates to…well, everything.

While the previous chapters placed a rather direct emphasis on the importance of fitness through knowledge, nutrition, and self-discovery, the focus of this chapter will call upon your ability to consider things from various *selfless* perspectives; a stepping stone to a healthy body and mind. Our ability to consider alternative perspectives compels us to consider the entirety of virtually every process—including, but not limited to, our commitment to an optimal level of personal performance.

As we have already discussed, it is truly amazing what a slight shift in perspective can do for us. After all, small changes can really add up. This slight shift can, and very often does, result in our ability to better understand the things we must *do* in order to succeed. As our understanding increases, we are better able to go "all-in" or fully commit to virtually any goal. The essence of this philosophy shapes our increasing ability to "fall in love with the process" of achievement, to allow the process to arise within us.

Give Love a Chance

The concept of "falling in love" connects us with a deep sense of personal commitment—a state of mind where we actually begin to discover how our goals and objectives can quickly become our passions, and ultimately, our achievements. The power of this concept creates a state of mind that brings us into alignment with the universal law of attraction. Let's face it—falling in love with anything (or *anyone* for that matter) can be difficult if there is no apparent attraction. So what are we to do when we *know* something is good for us (exercise, nutrition, discipline, behavioral changes, etc.) but have little incentive on taking the action necessary to bring about our objectives?

Take a moment to recall the last time you celebrated an achievement. My hunch is that you can smile knowing how good it felt as you crossed the finish line of your goal. Now think about how you got there. Chances are someone did not take you by the hand and lead you to your achievement. While someone or something may have had an influence, you most likely worked for it using some kind of process or methodology. In other words, you tapped into something that ignited your passion, which fueled your drive, which compelled you into action! You discovered your *why* and, before you even realized it, you were falling in love with the process.

Achieving any goal requires us to implement a process that involves preparation, work ethic, determination, and a dose of tenacity. At first glance, these elements may seem difficult. But the work doesn't have to be miserable. In fact, evidence shows that most high-achievers actually *enjoy* the process despite working harder than most everyone else. How do they do it? Well, very often it is all a matter of perspective.

Perspective Changes Everything

Tapping into the power of *why* we do things creates an entirely new state of mind that virtually erases almost every negative thought or emotion associated with the process of achievement—those elements that are considered by everyone else to be "work." Our *why* compels us to see things different. The unique perspective allows us to begin associating *the process* with *the achievement*. The more this happens the more we are inclined to *fall in love* with the process. Suddenly, it seems as though our contempt for work becomes a passion for doing whatever it takes to reach our goal or objective.

> *"Falling in love is easy. Staying in love requires work."*

When our belief system is challenged, our ego typically assumes a defensive posture. No one enjoys the notion of being wrong, so the ego (the emotional defender) steps in to protect our core beliefs. It quickly rejects any notion of change, unwilling to admit the possibility that maybe there *is* a better approach. The ego denies any possibility of a better way of doing things with an assuring and rather familiar self-dialogue: "That's the way we've always done it. Besides, it works, so why should we change?"

Personally speaking, coming to grips with the concept of *falling in love* with the process was difficult for me to understand at first. You see, I was programmed at a relatively early age to *fight* for everything I set out to accomplish. The tactic worked most of the time. The results of my traditional methods cast a "work hard" mindset I later found difficult to release when the concept of falling in love crossed my path. I later learned that it is often difficult to consider an alternative approach to success when our current methodologies are actually working. So, if my methods were working, why would I ever consider changing them? The simple truth is that I was sick and tired of having to work so hard *despite* my success.

When my mentor first introduced the concept of falling in love with the process, he was actually trying to show me how I could continue achieving great things while actually *enjoying* the process. As foreign as it was for me to initially conceive, I have to admit how empowering it was when I put into place the new processes to pursue my dreams, goals, and aspirations. Instead of "paying a price" for success, I actually started to *enjoy* the price of success. What a refreshing concept!

The self-imposed pressures now removed, I could feel myself breathe deeper, focus more, and settle into a ritual I enjoyed. I was suddenly better able to slow my mind and allow the moments of my life to wash over me. I was no longer burdened by the stressors that typically accompany a "work hard" mindset. I cannot recall a more gratifying time in my entire life. I believe you, too, will discover the same enriching experience as you adopt this simple yet powerful concept.

Finding the "Fun" in the Dysfunction

A few months after adopting my new mindset, I decided to participate in a regional triathlon relay race. Admittedly, I was curious to experience this now relatively new concept in a competitive environment. My mind raced as I wondered whether I would be inclined to revert to my former *tough work* mindset.

I began to notice something new in my training regimen as I prepared for the race. There was an element of fun and desire mixed with underlying satisfaction and a bit of anxiety. While I had always considered the workout phase as a necessary evil, it had never occurred to me that it could also be an *enjoyable* aspect to the process. Make no mistake, my workouts still had purpose, and they were still grueling, but the entire process had shifted from a necessary chore to an invigorating experience with a completely different outlook. *Fun* had actually become a part of the process.

As race day arrived, I was overcome with an increasingly familiar calm confidence I had never experienced. Something was different. *I* was different. I felt an indescribable transformation in my competitive nature. Previously, my race days were filled with self-doubt, pressure, and anxiety as I secretly wondered whether I was adequately prepared. The transformation I experienced had given me the freedom to be fully present in the moment. I felt more clarity, confidence, and an unmistakable connection with my surroundings, not to mention my purpose. I was ready, and I proved it with one of the best performances of my life to that point. To top it all off, I could actually detect the energy of my competitors as well. I can remember it all with complete clarity as if it were a moment ago.

A Powerful Process

There is an increasing level of empowerment that exists as we learn to fall in love with the process of achievement. My personal empowerment came from an ability to consider an alternative approach to achievement through acceptance. Yours may come from a completely different source. It is fair to say, however, that love from *any* point of origin is a game-changer you should give serious consideration to if you're looking to realign yourself with your purpose while accelerating your results.

> *"We only get one shot at life. Seize the power, and make it the best shot of your life."*

The best reward for me along this transformational journey of self-discovery was also an unexpected one. My biggest supporter in *every* aspect of my life is my husband. During the course of supporting my efforts to embrace love as a basis for my own achievements, he too was absorbing the concept brilliantly. I'd like to say it was a complete surprise to realize he would embrace the perspective, but then again, my husband never ceases to impress me. I have watched him take control of his health in a way I have never seen before in our twenty-plus years together. It's as if he suddenly made friends with his health and they are having *fun* together. I've never seen him so enthusiastic about his health and of life in general. And I must admit, the results are rather impressive and contagious.

There is a power you can tap into which will provide an effortless and systematic transition to a healthier and happier you. All you have to do is allow yourself to utilize its amazing simplicity. We all have the capability to love the energy that will become us, the energy we use to give back, and the energy that defines us at any given moment in time.

A love-centric approach aligns you with your passion and will lead you to a radical transformation resulting in the achievement of virtually *anything* you set out to accomplish.

SECTION TWO

Mind

by
Gary Westfal

CHAPTER 1

A State of Mind

An External Examination of Our Internal Processes

The nature of our mind is an amazing concept to consider. It is physical, yet it is metaphysical. Memories, images, ideas, inspiration, dreams, and the epicenter for regulating our vital, life-sustaining processes (every second of every day, without fail) all happen because of the physical organism that governs these functions—our brain.

The power of the human mind is irrefutable, yet we hear this fact so often we fail to truly grasp the infinite potential that is readily available to us in the context of the message. We have been studying the mind long before the dawn of modern record keeping and have yet to discover its limits. Compare the mind to man's most sophisticated attempt at information processing—the computer. The average computer (as of this writing) can hold about 250,000 pictures, 20,000 songs, and hundreds of full-length videos, while our minds can perform an estimated *ten quadrillion* operations *per second*. Many of these processes happen without us having to consciously think about performing them. These processes are driven by our subconscious mind. Amazing! But of all the things our subconscious mind *can* do, there is one thing it absolutely *cannot* do—determine fact from fiction.

What is a Mind?

In considering the abilities of the mind, one of the basic questions we should ask ourselves at the outset is, "*What is a mind?*" As fundamental as this question may seem, it is not as easily answered as we may initially think. While we all have a mind, it is hidden—for the most part—and is not prone to physical examination even inasmuch as our actual brain.

There are more scientific and psychological theories and conjecture centered on the topic of the human mind than there are actual known facts about it. Nevertheless, our fascination with the mind has led to some amazing breakthroughs on the capabilities and diversities of the mind, which have given us a better understanding of this rather complex aspect of ourselves. For example, we've learned there are in fact *three* components of the mind—the *conscious, subconscious,* and *unconscious.*

The concept of the three levels of the mind is nothing new. The differences between each aspect of the mind are subtle but distinct. Each has an effect on the other. Understanding each of the aspects of the mind allows us to better understand ourselves from more than one perspective.

The *conscious mind* is what most of us associate with who we are, because that is where most of us live day to day. The conscious mind is distinguished by its ability for awareness, but it is by no means where all the action takes place. Nor is it *always* aware, in the truest sense of the word, as the subconscious is also capable of its own level of awareness.

The conscious mind communicates to the outside world and the inner self through various means (thoughts, words, feelings, emotions, judgments, and actions) and to the subconscious mind by most of the very same methods. In other words, the subconscious mind is watching and learning all the time, but for the most part, tends to have a "mind" of its own. Of all the functions the conscious mind is capable of, none is more significant or powerful than its ability to perceive reality, as we know it. On the other hand, the subconscious mind is simply unable to determine reality, and instead, accepts and stores the data that it is fed by the conscious mind as an *experience*. This is powerful insight we can use to change virtually any area of our life by simply reprogramming our subconscious mind to accept a fresh, new mindset.

The subconscious mind takes everything literally. It stores all of our recent (short-term) memories and is in continual contact with both the conscious and unconscious minds. It is easily manipulated by a dominant, strong-willed conscious mind and will respond accordingly, regardless of whether its programming benefits the psychological sanity of its host. So be careful of the thoughts you dwell upon, because your subconscious is listening and learning all the time.

The subconscious mind is always on alert, no matter what state of consciousness we are in and is therefore largely responsible for the maintenance and health functions of our body—our heartbeat, circulation, digestion process, etc. The subconscious is infinite intelligence collected across the traditional boundaries of time and space. It helps us to receive new thoughts, ideas, and insight compounded upon the precepts man has collected over the years of his existence. A thought that is accepted as a truth by the conscious mind will be *automatically* executed by the subconscious. So again, be mindful of your thoughts.

We know there is a distinct difference between our conscious and subconscious minds, but what is the difference between the subconscious and *unconscious*? Even some so-called experts in the field of psychology struggle with the difference between the subconscious and unconscious minds and have also been known to use the two interchangeably. The unconscious mind should not be confused with an unconscious *physical state* that is associated with being knocked out or anesthetized, although both definitions do have similarities.

Think of the unconscious mind as the deepest part of your psychological self. It is the storehouse of all your deep-seated emotions that have been programmed since birth. A traumatic childhood event is an example. Most of these thoughts are ones that have been repressed or simply forgotten over time but are still very much a part of you. Memories that are stored in our unconscious mind are almost impossible to access by the conscious mind. The principle difference between your unconscious and subconscious minds is that the *unconscious* mind is the source of all the programs your subconscious mind uses.

Want to make a real and lasting change in your life? It is your unconscious mind (programming) that you must work on. In order to do that, you must begin on the *conscious* level by taking control of your thoughts and directing your focus in such a way that those thoughts influence what programs your subconscious uses. There are many ways to go about doing that of course, but one of the best methods comes by way of awareness. Without awareness we remain blind to the fact that change is required. Once awareness emerges, however, everything changes. Awareness brings about insight and introspection, and provides an opportunity for us to begin building a framework for making the changes we desire for our lives.

Our mind is an intricate configuration of many complicated and specific functions simultaneously occurring on all three echelons, but its foremost feature is that of consciousness. The mind orchestrates and categorizes every mental experience we have, from logic and reasoning to the almost inexplicable nature of emotion. Human consciousness, more than anything, sets us apart from everything else in the world. Consciousness is so often connected to *perception*. Perception is personally defined, and, as such, presents a vague generality that offers little in terms of something that is in agreement, even between like-minded individuals.

Consciousness is most closely associated with *knowing*. Our knowing is directly connected to our experiences. Those experiences that bring about a *full awareness* are the best we've got in terms of providing an acceptable definition of consciousness. Experience, therefore, is the essence of knowing something.

Sometimes consciousness is directed outward, toward our environment—a sunset, the captivating behavior of children at play, and peaceful, serene landscapes for example. Other times it is directed inward—the refection of a memory or a conscious awareness of the present moment. This inward refection is called *self-awareness* or introspection. Both perspectives have immense value in shaping our experiences and thus increasing our self-awareness in support of our quest to know ourselves better.

As pointed out earlier, it is generally believed and scientifically substantiated that our subconscious minds *cannot* tell the difference between reality and alter-reality or what is real and what is not. The subconscious mind operates and reacts based on the thoughts we consciously program into it. It doesn't draw distinctions between realistic and unrealistic expectations.

43

Our ability to program our subconscious minds is an *amazingly* simple process, yet few people know this. Why? They are simply *unaware*.

> *"The filter of our biases and beliefs govern the limits of our imaginations, and hence the programming of our subconscious."*

We can effectively rewire the synapses that perpetuate the programming our biases allow to pass through its filtering process governing our beliefs. In other words, we can change *what* and *how* we think in an instant. This is profound. Understanding this insight will empower you far beyond the prescriptive nature of the information it presents. Your ability to understand and apply this knowledge will also lead you to experience the beginning of what is undoubtedly the source of true happiness—knowing yourself. At its most elementary level, *self*-awareness involves an awareness of what your body is doing physically or mechanically (walking, talking, running). At a higher level, it involves a *functional* awareness. This level speaks more to being in tune with your physical health. Think of it as knowing yourself better than the doctors know you. Higher yet, it involves an awareness of your own mortality.

Albert Einstein said it best in his personal credo, circa 1932, when he wrote...

> "The most beautiful and deepest experience a man can have is the sense of the mysterious...
>
> To sense that behind anything that can be experienced there is a something our minds cannot grasp and whose beauty and simplicity are but a feeble reflection..."

Live Consciously

How do you see the world? If you're like most people, you see the world through the lens of your own unique perspective, which is biased by two things: your past experiences and your future expectations. If we are to bring real and meaningful change to our lives we must change the way we look at life. So how do we do that? The answer is to live consciously.

Consider the most common example of driving home from a familiar place only to find that, once you have arrived, you have no recollection of a single moment of the journey. The most likely reason for this can be found in our tendency to escape the present for preoccupying, predominant thoughts of the mind— either of the past, or of the future. Why is it so easy for our minds to become preoccupied with these thoughts, most of which serve little to no use to us whatsoever?

"The true measure of any society is not what it knows but what it does with what it knows."
~ Warren Bennis

The loudest and most influential voice you hear is your own inner voice, your self-critic. It can work for or against you, depending on the messages you allow. It can be optimistic or pessimistic. It can wear you down or cheer you on. You control the sender and the receiver, but only if you consciously take responsibility for and control over your inner conversation.

The problem is not the mind; the problem is our *identification* with it. We believe we are a product of our thoughts. Nothing could be further from the truth. Our thoughts define the exposure of our experiences. They will forever be etched upon the slate of our subconscious mind but serve only as a record

45

of our experiences. The problem arises when we become so preoccupied with our thoughts that we essentially rob ourselves of what lies before us—the present. It is the present moment that holds the most value in life. It is where everything occurs in its purest state. So, how do we arrest these dominating thoughts and operate in the present?

Dissociate. A dissociation of the mind gradually allows us to *dis-identify* with the controlling nature of thought. We can dissociate by watching our thoughts. You should consciously watch over your thoughts. Be mindful to be aware of what is happening inside of you while rejecting whatever is useless and accepting what is good to enhance the quality of your life.

Watch the mind—*be* the watcher and let the mind be watched, witnessed, and observed. The mind is always going somewhere else; it never wants to be *here*. Because if the mind is *here* it is no longer needed. In the present there is no need for the mind—consciousness is enough. The mind is needed only somewhere else in the future or the past, but never here. Therefore, when you walk, just walk, but be alert. Converse or communicate, but be alert and engaged. Stop allowing your mind to run all over the world. Be here, *now*.

> *"So, the single most vital step on your journey toward enlightenment is this: learn to dis-identify from your mind. Every time you create a gap in the stream of mind, the light of your consciousness grows stronger. One day you may catch yourself smiling at the voice in your head, as you would smile at the antics of a child. This means that you no longer take the content of your mind all that seriously, as your sense of self does not depend on it."*
> ~ Eckhart Tolle, *The Power of Now*

If you *watch* the movement of thoughts going on inside you it is not difficult to keep those thoughts pure. And it is not difficult to recognize impure thoughts (those that create a sense of restlessness inside you) and the thoughts that create a flow of peace. Those that bring joy are pure, while those that create any kind of disturbance or restlessness are impure. You must avoid impure thoughts. And if you constantly watch your mind, your thoughts will become more and more pure.

A great and radical change happens through observation. Our mind functions far more efficiently when we observe it because all that is irrelevant falls away. As a result, our mind ceases to carry unnecessary weight and, in essence, becomes light. As we learn to become a watcher, the mind is able to rest. Remember, it is your identification with the thoughts in your mind that gives them life. The mind contains all your misery, all your wounds. Your consciousness has no wounds. Your consciousness knows nothing of misery. Your consciousness is innocent and the one true resting place of happiness and contentment. In dis-identifying with the mind, you are not constrained to seeing yourself as the mind would like you to believe. You are not at the mercy of what the mind is telling you about yourself, about others, or about the world around you. You do not have to do what the mind tells you to do nor must you have to *be* who the mind tells you to be.

The Power of the Mind

Each and every one of us is inherently programmed with the ability to reason. With every choice we face, we weigh the reasons to act or the reasons to resist. In other words, the things that motivate us are driven, in large part, by two emotions: a

47

desire to *gain* something or a desire to *protect* something. With every decision comes an internal evaluation of what the results of our decisions will bring us or how it will protect us. We quickly evaluate whether something we face is worth taking action on or avoiding altogether. The current position of our life has largely been defined by the manner in which we generally approach these kinds of decisions.

Do you allow distractions to easily influence you away from a better, or more productive, choice? Do you allow the memories of a painful past to dominate your thoughts? Would you rather sleep in than get up an hour early, only to complain there's just not enough time during the day to do the things that bring change (and successful results) into your life? Are you taking on too many things at once, effectively reducing the focus and spreading yourself too thin because of your ad hoc approach to life's priorities and activities? Are you leading with your emotions, reacting to life instead of watching the wonder of life unfold before you?

> *"The mind is a powerful force. It can enslave us or empower us. It can plunge us into the depths of misery or take us to the heights of ecstasy. Learn to use the power wisely."*
> ~ David Cuschieri

Humans are motivated by getting, having, and keeping what we need and want. The *getting* and *having* aspect of that statement are force multipliers in terms of bringing us to a point of action, whereas the *keeping* aspect of the statement very often *prevents* us from gaining or experiencing even more because of an underlying fear of potential loss. So how do we "fix" this?

The trick to correcting the conditions keeping us stuck in a state of perpetual stagnation and fear—the cycle that tends to frustrate us the most—is to tap into the convincing strength of our subconscious. All too often our reasons for *not* doing something are simply stronger than our reasons *for* doing it. If we could find a way to reverse the process we would be so much better off, wouldn't we? Well, the simple truth is, it's easier than you may think.

To put everything into perspective, one of the first things we should consider doing is to consciously *allow* ourselves to succeed. Giving ourselves permission to succeed penetrates the subconscious with programming that ignites a process of new ideas and reasons for acting on behalf of our desires. We will always have some level of anxiety, feeding our desire to procrastinate. "Maybe if I put it off for just a little longer, it won't be as bad," we tell ourselves. But what if I told you the power of choice is so strong, once it is enacted, it initiates a process that shocks the subconscious and ignites forces of change allowing you to escape circumstance and create the life you want? Do I have your attention now?

> *"The energy of the mind is the essence of life."*
> ~ Aristotle

Imagination Will Set You Free

Freedom begins in the mind. The mind is a place where we can escape to create anything we can imagine. Imagination leads to insight, which leads to introspection, which leads to discovery, which leads to change! *Real* change takes place when we allow ourselves the liberty to put aside bias and preconceived notions long enough to be fascinated with what our innermost selves are telling us.

I've said it time and again: don't be so *judgmental* about the things your mind—or your imagination—is trying to reveal to you. Doing so only prevents you from realizing the truest potential for happiness and fulfillment you can expect to discover in this life. One of the most difficult things to do is withhold judgment and yield to the variety of possibilities and discovery that lie within us.

Most of us are programmed to be skeptical, judgmental, and cautious. Oftentimes, our cognitive filters prevent us from accepting the raw information provided by our imagination. We consciously and selectively accept or deny information based on the learned perception of our predispositions. In other words, if it *makes sense*, we retain it. If it doesn't, we're quick to write it off as unrealistic or unobtainable. The result is a tragic disruption of the natural flow of ideas, imagination, and insight that point directly toward the full experience we expect from life. Don't allow it to happen! Instead, listen to the sounds, grab the images, and feel the *richness* that is literally already a part of you.

If you have difficulty connecting with your seemingly elusive insight, you're not alone, and you're *not* abnormal. It may take some time to recognize the creative activity, but when it happens, you will know it…and your world will come alive as it did when you were a child listening to fairytales and stories. You will begin to see things in their raw form and will be fascinated by the simplicity of it all.

Look closely at the wonder and amazement of a child as they process the sheer amount of information and sensory input of life. You can tell the young ones anything! When you do, their imaginations come alive and conjure images and limitless possibilities. We tend to lose that as we "mature" into adulthood. We become jaded, skeptical, and *realistic*…what's that about anyway? For that matter, what exactly is "real"? I'm here to tell you that "real" is anything we decide to make it. Are your dreams, goals, and aspirations real? If they're not real yet, then begin to *imagine* them to be. Allow your imagination to show you things and begin to make them real in your life. Once they reveal themselves to you, crystallize them in your mind. Feel the passion and excitement that begins to well within. Focus on it with all you've got. Call it into your life, believing that it is your destiny to have it, to hold it, to experience it. And don't ever allow *anyone* to convince you that it is unrealistic.

Napoleon Hill wrote, "Whatever the mind of man can conceive and believe, it can achieve." What is *your* mind telling you to believe? What are some of the possibilities that are still a part of you that you have put aside?

Can you imagine what life would be like without the many things that were once but a glimmer of an imaginative thought in someone's mind? Pick literally anything that is a convenience, a conveyance, or a contraption and you'll know exactly what I'm talking about.

Imagination in its most basic form comes from the storytellers. J. K. Rowling immediately comes to mind because her stories are so fascinating and profound. Had she not imagined the things supporting the Harry Potter series, we would never have such wonderful stories to share with each other, especially our children.

Rowling's stories are a testament to the wild and vivid imagination she has and the manner in which she can express it. Because she had the courage to yield to her imagination and call it forth, and care for it and work for it, we now have the pleasure of knowing such possibilities could exist. Such stories are inspirational and ignite an unending array of other inspiring aspects that perpetuate far beyond the narrative of *her* storyline, to the possibilities that exist within yours. There is some insight here when you consider how imagination is sparked by a former imagination. A single drop of creative thought can form a waterfall of enlightenment as it moves through time.

The Three-Legged Stool

Striving to "get it right" in life typically amounts to achieving some sort of balance. Our lives are broadly defined by the three aspects of our physical, emotional, and spiritual well-being. If any one of the "legs" of our stool (life) is shorter (deficient) than the other, we experience imbalance to some varying degree, depending upon just how short or deficient it is.

Life is dynamic and is always in a state of motion. It is not static. It waits for no one. It is not a respecter of persons and will continue to perpetuate long after we are gone. This is a truth. There is no middle ground. With this in mind, we are wise to understand that we are all on the same "ride." How we choose to define the experiences of that ride is left to the greatest power we have as human beings—our power of choice.

We are either growing or declining, which is to say, we are constantly changing. We are defined by our choices, and therefore have the power to choose whether we are growing or declining and to what extent. What makes life so perplexing for some is that they must make conscious choices to experience growth, while opting for the alternative is almost a "no-brainer" and so much easier.

When a carpenter designs a stool he goes to great lengths to ensure the measurements are accurate, the materials are strong, and the plans are in place to support a result that will allow the stool to fulfill its purpose. If anything is out of sync, the stool will not be able to function properly. There will be imbalance, dysfunction, and deterioration that, unless corrected, will lead to the eventual demise of the stool, relegating it to the scrap heap.

Our lives are a lot like the three-legged stool. If all three legs are strong, we end up with a structure that supports the purpose for which it is intended. A strong stool can take a lot of pressure before it breaks. A well-built stool is akin to a well-balanced life— it is stable, therefore we rest in the knowledge that all three areas of our lives are congruent with one another and will support us when we need it most.

Make a choice, starting today, to bring your life into balance. Make a conscious choice to listen to something other than the inside of your head. Use each of your senses as you move through life. Choose to experience the richness of life as it exists, *right now.* Savor the aroma of freshly brewed coffee, look directly into the eyes of the person talking with you, taste your food as it hits your pallet. Conscious living begins with a choice you can freely make…if you are aware.

CHAPTER 2

Master Mind

Awakening the Process of Self-Awareness

Balance and harmony are key essentials in the way our mind interacts with the physical and spiritual aspects of who we are. Our mind serves as a filter by interpreting messages sent to it by our physical and spiritual bodies. As we progress toward awareness and release the stories we live by, our mind becomes increasingly clearer and more efficient at revealing the things we need to see and learn as we get closer to becoming who we really are. Our increasing ability to *master the mind* is where the "magic" happens.

> ***"Our life is the creation of our mind."***
> ~ Buddhist scripture

Many of us spend time and energy taking care of our physical bodies as we continually try to find ways to look and feel younger. And, while that's certainly a great approach to a sensible balance of life, it is nonetheless incomplete. While we are, for the most part, well aware of the condition of our physical body, we generally tend to come up short on the health and well-being of our mind. When it comes to taking care of our mind, we tend to treat it as more of an afterthought (pardon the pun) rather than an essential component to what completes us. All too often we think of the mind as something that is *outside* our control when in fact, it is just the opposite.

Developing a healthy mindset is critical to building a life that is defined by *your* terms. Not all happiness is created equal. Staying true to your version or definition of happiness makes all the difference in terms of whether you find peace or pressure in your quest to master your mind. In fact, researchers[1] have recently discovered a link to the *type* of happiness you seek and say it can make a big difference in your long-term well-being. Their findings tell us what philosophers have known all along— *enduring happiness* is inextricably linked to having a larger, longer-lasting purpose or sense of meaning in life, whereas pleasure-seeking happiness is not. It makes sense if you think about it.

This section of the book will reveal ways for us to increasingly master our mind. The manner and degree to which you choose to incorporate the concepts of this book into your life will determine what you gain from the practice. You can make a conscious choice to learn to refine the filter that is your mind and make your mind work *for* you (rather than against you) in each waking moment by increasing your self-awareness and learning when to listen and when to allow it to roam in search of dreams, goals, and aspirations.

---

1 UCLA Newsroom (http://newsroom.ucla.edu/releases/don-t-worry-be-happy-247644)

Managing Thought Noise

When was the last time you sat in quiet contemplation without a barrage of extraneous thoughts bombarding your mind? For that matter, when was the last time you sat *anywhere* without the constant chaos of thoughts competing for your attention? Let's face it—the majority of thoughts we typically have serve little to no value to us whatsoever. Most thoughts we have are distractors based on illusions of what *should* have been or *could* have been, or they are so outlandishly ridiculous their only rightful place is on the pages of some poorly contrived fantasy novel. Where do these thoughts *come* from anyway? More importantly, how can we arrest them to make room for the *emptiness* that precedes insight, introspection, and inspiration?

Emptiness is the absence of thought noise. It is a powerful state of mind that is achieved with practice and patience. Emptiness allows us to discern that still, quiet voice of reason, inspiration, and insight leading to empowering, uplifting thoughts that *should* occupy our mind.

When the mind is quiet it is better able to detect subtle communication across all three of our aspect planes—body, mind, and spirit. Yes, the mind even communicates with *itself* through both the productive and unproductive thought processes we just covered. Our objective is to ensure that a clear channel for *productive* communication increasingly takes place by mastering the process by which it is achieved. So how do we do this? By *breathing*.

The process of breathing is typically a natural bodily function we take for granted. We inhale and exhale without ever really giving it much thought, unless for some reason, we suddenly find ourselves short of breath or unable to breathe freely.

Each breath we take is a gift of life. One highly effective method of reducing thought noise is to focus on our breathing. *Conscious* breathing is what most experts will prescribe as a way to realign our attention to the present moment. For example, spiritual leaders teach students to focus on breathing as they begin meditation. Furthermore, experiments have shown the Vagus nerve is stimulated by regular, deep-focused breaths, causing a calming of mental and physical activity—a scientific link between the breath and the mind.

Reducing Thought Noise through Conscious Breathing – Three Steps

Step 1: Identify/recognize the noise. We have become so used to our thoughts drifting in and out that we have come to regard them as normal occurrences. Most of us are hardly aware how much we actually allow our minds to drift until we consider the fact that we have little to no recollection of an entire journey, say, between home and work or a page read in a book. (Are you still consciously reading?) An overactive mind robs us of the full experience of life in the present moment. Until we become aware of the dominance our thoughts have over us, we remain a slave to our thoughts and are unable to reduce the frequency of the occurrences. However, once we begin to recognize just how much it is occurring, we gain an upper hand.

"What consumes your mind controls your life."

Step 2: Address the noise directly (command it to stop). Although it may sometimes seem impossible, we have the power to control our thoughts. Why is it that this statement seems so absurd to some people? I often hear people telling me how they just can't understand how their thoughts race or how they just *cannot* stop thinking. My typical response is to smile and tell them they have the power to control their thoughts as easily as they have the power to turn off the lights or the television.

Let's not overthink this. The fact is we can all stop useless thoughts from overpowering our mind by simply commanding them to stop. Those who think otherwise haven't yet realized the power they have relinquished to their thoughts, and, until they reclaim that power, their thoughts will continue to dominate their life.

Try this—next time you catch your thoughts drifting away uncontrollably, command them (either audibly or in your conscious mind) to stop. When you do, use an authoritative voice your subconscious recognizes and respects. Then, immediately force yourself to recognize something about the present moment. Acknowledge the sights and sounds that surround you. If you're meditating or trying to fall asleep, focus on your breathing by following the guidance in Step 3 below.

Let us also consider a light-hearted congenial relationship with the mind rather than a command and control one. It is okay to be amused at the wandering mind, as it does not create resistance or irritation. Develop an "Oh, I see what you're doing. Nice try!" approach.

Step 3: Focus on breathing. Take a slow, conscious inhalation through the nose followed by a slight pause, followed by a controlled exhalation through the mouth. This method serves to call upon a focus that aligns us with procedure while preparing the mind for meditation as we escape the extraneous and distracting thoughts that preoccupy our mind. Focus on goodness flowing into the body as you draw a breath, and then think of the exhalation as ridding the body of all that is unclean or no longer useful.

A proper breathing technique allows us to focus and calls upon our highest power to summon our greatest strength—awareness. The power of awareness realigns us with the present moment. It is the present moment that contains the absolute purest form of life, as we know it to be, *right now*. We have so much power in the present moment, yet all too often we allow the thought noise of the past or the future to obscure the magic or the essence of the moment. Consider the following story of a military special operator who made it through a life-or-death situation by using the power of focus through conscious breathing, as narrated from his first-person perspective:

"I was coming in and out of consciousness when I realized I was being transported from an H-60 Blackhawk helicopter to an awaiting vehicle. I had no idea where I was. The only thing I can remember is the searing pain that went through my chest as the bullet entered my right lung. I must have blacked out shortly thereafter because the next thing I remember was being transported into the vehicle once we had landed. Thoughts of my family and my life raced through my mind. *Is this how it all ends?* I thought as I heard someone telling me to breathe—*commanding* me to breathe.

"I vaguely recall how damn difficult it was to take a breath. After all, my right lung had collapsed because there was a chunk of lead lodged in it, preventing me from taking a full breath. I tried *so* hard to breathe I must have passed out, because the next thing I remember was a pretty rough ride through town as the two special operators raced to get me to the nearest medical facility—a makeshift surgical office atop the desk of an on-call flight surgeon in the basement of a nearby outpost in Burkina Faso, West Africa.

"To this day, I'm not exactly certain how we made it through the embattled streets of the city with the efficiency we did, but if not for the heroic actions of the two unknown special operators commanding me to breathe, I never would've made it. My mind wanted to focus more on the trauma I had experienced and on the memories of what I had to lose instead of what I had to gain by fighting to live. I was, in essence, preparing to die by reliving every memory I could get my mind to recall. Instead, my focus on breathing summoned an indescribable power I had not previously known. By focusing on my breathing, I managed to let go of the past as I made a decision right then and there to do the best I could to live. I'm here today because I decided to put all of myself—my entire being—into helping to save my own life."

The story above is an extreme example of the power of focused breathing. Though, if one man can help save his own life through the power of sheer will using this *one* method of focus, then you can do the same in virtually *any* area of your life using the very same technique. Thought noise *can* be controlled. Don't allow it to rob you of what is right in front of you at any given moment. Conscious breathing is the first step in getting there. I can assure you that the man in the story experienced a super-consciousness few of us have encountered, but all of us have access to, if we will only seek to discover it.

Meditate – One of the best ways to reduce thought noise is to meditate. Yet, for most of us, the very act of meditation actually gives *rise* to the noise that dominates our minds. So what are we to do? How can we arrest the noise that is drowning out our ability to meditate?

We are vibrational matches to our surroundings and our beliefs. Therefore, one of the methods I routinely prescribe is to use ambient sound to help block out whatever is going on around you. Ambient sound, often referred to as white noise, can be anything from the steady sound of waves crashing along a shoreline to a specific frequency generated by a CD, or a source specifically designed to help reduce distractions. Avoid listening to anything with lyrics. Lyrics subtly draw our minds into interpreting the words and distract us from concentrating on emptiness, essentially defeating the purpose.

White noise can help us move from a distracted state of mind to one more conducive for meditating and entering a zone of nothingness—a zone of ultimate relaxation—where the mind can rejuvenate and replenish. One of the best sounds we can focus on is the sound of water. For some, it is of waves crashing along a shoreline as mentioned earlier. For others, it is the gentle and peaceful sound of water running along its path, like in a brook or stream. Some people use the sacred sound of *Om*—largely touted to be the vibration of the universe—to reduce thought noise and transition into meditation. Om is said to be the frequency that connects and joins all things. Om is a sound we can generate by using the lowest frequency of our own voice, resonating a vibration in our throat and chest. *Ommmmmmm...*is a lingering sound that flows like energy itself. It is a sound most frequently associated with Tibetan monks as they meditate.

Opening ourselves to the vibration of Om grounds us to the Earth and to the boundless nature of the universe. If that's a bit too cosmic for you then perhaps you're just not ready for this practice. Don't sweat it; just don't be too quick to discount the benefits of meditation…no matter what it takes to get there. Whatever method you choose to reduce or eliminate thought noise should be one that works best for you.

Once you experience the power of meditation you will have created a connection to a source that you will desire to revisit often. The practice of meditation eventually becomes a way to investigate your mind and change the perspective you have of the world. You're not tuning *out* so much as tuning *up* your brain, improving your self-monitoring skills. Meditation brings our presence to the absence of thought—*nothingness*—where true *nonjudgmental* awareness resides. It is where the purest form of *right now* exists. And it is an experience that is life changing.

> **"Knowing yourself is the beginning of all wisdom."**
> ~ Aristotle

Let go of expectations – Clinging to our expectations prevents us from seeing alternative possibilities. It also places us in closer proximity to the elements of fear. Think of the times in your life when things didn't work out quite the way you thought they would. Chances are, things actually worked out *better* than you expected, even if not perfectly aligned with the timeline or concept of your expectations.

All too often our expectations set us up for disappointment through the thought noise that dominates our mind. We build expectations of what other people *should* do, what our lives *should* be like, and how situations *should* (ideally) work out…and yet, things rarely ever come close to what we perceive should happen.

Trade your expectations for gratitude. That's right, *gratitude*. A grateful mind aligns us with the present moment and the power of awareness. Gratitude allows us to accept life (and reality) the way it is, right now. It opens our eyes to *what is* instead of what may (or may never) be.

Exercise – Most physical fitness regimens, no matter how intense, have proven to reduce thought noise by releasing chemicals that provide a calming effect, therefore relaxing the brain. Walking or jogging outdoors provides the mind with a great deal of sensory distraction that provides an increased blood flow to your entire body, not to mention the sights, scents, and sounds that are peaceful distractors to an overactive mind.

Your body produces endorphins during strenuous physical activity, providing a natural morphine-like chemical reaction in the brain that is actually healthy. When endorphins are released into the bloodstream they diminish pain while triggering euphoria, or positive feelings. Endorphin release varies from person to person, which simply means all bodies are not created equal. Therefore, two people conducting the same workout routine will produce different levels of endorphin secretion. Despite that, however, the benefits of exercise and associated endorphin release have been shown to produce a healthy benefit for calming and clarity of the mind. Personally speaking, I get some of my best ideas for writing or speaking during the middle of my workouts.

Rediscover your balance – The expression of our desires is another key to overcoming thought noise. We all have something that we can identify as a true calling. Find out *who* you truly are. Then, simply embrace what you discover as you concentrate on the positive aspects and expectations associated with your purpose.

Sometimes, unhappiness emanates from a source that brings about inner conflict with where we are versus where we believe we should be in terms of our calling in life. In other words, our story can sometimes be in conflict with where we believe our lives should be. If this describes you, relax. Don't beat yourself up over it. Instead, rest knowing that you have reached a significant breakthrough just by recognizing it. Now, what do we do about it?

I believe *all* the answers we seek reside within us, yet we consistently look for answers *outside* of ourselves. While some clues about who we are reveal themselves externally, the core truth resides within us. If you have yet to find your purpose or true calling in life, here's how to find it...

Ask.

Whoa, wait just a minute! It can't be that simple, can it? Indeed, it is. Now, some of you may want to debate this by telling me that you *have* been asking, but nothing seems to come to you. To that I say: you could be going about it incorrectly. You see, *asking* is just part of the formula. For, when you ask, you also have an obligation or responsibility to open your eyes (and your mind) to watch and listen for the answers that will reveal themselves. It is a universal law of nature.

> **"Ask and you shall receive."**
> ~ Matthew 7:7, the Bible

Once you ask, begin immediately paying attention to the cues and the clues that reveal themselves. Because this is a universal law of nature, there is no other alternative or course for the answers to take but to be driven straight out of the source—the very question you have asked. Amazing, isn't it? Test me on this and you, too, will discover how truly magical this concept is. And remember—every one of us has a purpose. Our purpose holds so many wonderful things for us if we would just begin to recognize the clues that lead to the discovery of it and begin to operate in the lane of that very purpose. So, how do we do that?

Begin by taking stock of what brings you joy. What drives you? What are you passionate about? What inherent gifts or abilities can you begin to develop? These are your initial cues leading to the core of your purpose. Spend some time on this, because it is one aspect of your life that will bring happiness, peace, and true contentment. You just cannot beat the return on your investment of time.

Realign your actions to happiness…to your passions. Are you *truly* happy doing what you are currently doing? Do your present circumstances support the calling of your passions? If so, tap into that power and allow it to feed you. If not, *change* it as soon as you practically can.

> *"Life is like riding a bicycle.*
> *To keep your balance, you must keep moving."*
> ~ Albert Einstein

Channel Your Emotions

Our thought processes are largely governed by two psychological components: logic and emotion. These components can, and often do, conflict with one another. Consider the experience of shopping for a new car.

You walk onto the car lot armed with an idea of the kind of vehicle you are looking for and a pre-determined limit on the amount of money you wish to spend. After you are greeted by the friendly salesperson, you begin looking at your choices and quickly discover how the limits of your budget have prevented you from considering more desirable (and expensive) models.

The salesperson convinces you that there is no harm in merely *looking* at the other vehicles and enticingly explains the safety features, benefits, and options offered by several of the higher priced models. You sit behind the wheel of a model just above your price range and imagine yourself driving this particular vehicle as you gradually begin to justify going beyond the limits of your budget.

The salesperson asks what it will take to put you into this "better" vehicle. The salesperson pauses for a moment, careful not to interrupt your imagination (emotion) and then "helps" alleviate your emotional turmoil by revealing the "slight" increase in your monthly payment required to close the deal (essentially calling upon your logic to help justify your emotions).

Your emotions soon begin to override the logic of your original plan. The irony is that you will attempt to use logic to justify your emotions in order to satisfy your desires for the higher-priced model. In the end, you will only be met with disappointment when you feel the sting of your ill-advised financial decision. Ugh…buyer's remorse!

Emotion is a *powerful* force. Because *so* many variables drive our emotions, we must strive to gain a deeper understanding of the role of our emotions. A deeper understanding leads to awareness. And awareness leads to our increasing ability to strike a *balance* between emotion and logic that works better in the broader perspective of our life. When you understand your own emotions, you are able to recognize them easier and will begin to respond to them differently. You will begin seeing situations differently, allowing you to act differently toward any circumstance.

Thought Processes

It is largely believed the pathway of our thoughts first travel through the limbic system of our brain and then to the Neocortex. While the limbic pathway serves to preserve memory, it is also a place where emotions are associated with virtually everything we are exposed to—images, scents, habits, behaviors, motivation, and, ah yes, words.

We are hard-wired to experience emotions first, leaving us hardly any time to logically process them before we react to them. If you think about it, our lives run primarily on the emotions we have learned to associate with virtually...*everything*. This programming is largely responsible for the relationships we have, from our most intimate to our most political. It's no wonder the world is in such a state of flux with emotions typically leading the way in the decision matrix. So what can we do about it?

Self-management builds upon a foundational skill of self-awareness. Self-awareness is absolutely necessary because we can only choose how to actively and effectively respond to an emotion if we are aware of it. Awareness gives us a very slight but *significant* edge in beating emotion to the finish line of conclusion. The significance speaks to our capability, while the "slight edge" speaks to the subtlety of the role and the precision with which our capabilities play in the process.

Look, the sad fact is that most people are simply unaware of their emotions until *after* they have reacted to them. This leads only to discord, discontent, and regret. Why settle for that scenario when you can create a positive and productive alternative?

Don't be the victim of an emotional hijacking. Instead, be quick to recognize your emotions as something that is designed to create a pre-arranged mindset that may not always be accurate. You can develop an ability to better recognize your emotions by connecting with the insight and intuition that resides within you through meditation, allowing you to be more mindful of how those emotions are influencing your behavior, now and into the future.

> *"I think, therefore I am."*
> ~ Rene' Descartes

The above quote, from the French philosopher, mathematician, and writer has stood the test of time and speaks to the power that our thoughts have in shaping our lives.

It's true our thoughts play a major role in shaping everything from the opinions we have of ourselves to the everyday decisions we make along the course of our lives. For if we limit those thoughts through fear (or any other self-deprecating method) then we affect the opportunities and experiences of life that are waiting for us.

If we could somehow get beyond the rational (and often limiting) thought processes that dominate our lives we would find that virtually anything is possible. But how do we do that? Well, one of the first things we have to do is shift our thinking away from the fact that failure is bad.

> *"...for I have learned more about success from failure than I have from the victories I have savored."*

That's a quote by yours truly. When it comes to success, one of the biggest lessons in *my* life has been to accept failure or "setbacks" for what they are—learning opportunities. It's not common practice for me to *seek* failure but I have learned to embrace it for everything it offers in the way of knowing what not to do inasmuch as I have learned what to do. The experiences have allowed me to accelerate my life in so many areas in spite of the number of setbacks that I've had the pleasure of experiencing.

Our minds tend to draw false generalizations based on isolated or past unpleasant events or occurrences. It assigns meaning to each one of those events in such a way that leaves an indelible mental imprint of "experience" the likes of which drive our perceptions, and thus our decisions going forward. It may come as no surprise, but it is up to us how we frame those experiences and store them in our subconscious minds.

Limiting beliefs prevent us from experiencing life at its fullest. Why then would any of us knowingly accept these thoughts? The short answer is that we wouldn't. But all too often, we either accept it as an inherent part of our reality or we begin to believe it is a part of who we are personally.

Want to get past this? Then first accept the fact that you can indeed change reality. That's right, reality is what you make of it. That may seem trite or overly simplistic, but the fact remains that you decide your own reality. Remember, our reality is shaped by how we process our experiences. Begin by processing your experiences through the lens of a limitless filter. Open your eyes to new experiences with an attitude of expectation over limitation, lack, and insufficiency.

To change your perception of reality and the acceptance of limiting beliefs being a natural part of your life, begin by changing the way you identify with destructive thoughts. Stop allowing yourself to be defined by limiting beliefs. If you think you'll never be financially independent, you never will be. Think about how powerful a statement that is.

If limiting beliefs have the power to prevent you from experiencing the goodness of life then it only seems logical that the opposite holds true. Removing the limits from our beliefs can only serve to open the aperture of perspective and opportunity that awaits us. For if you believe you can in fact become financially independent then it is also true.

Whatever you think you know is most likely a figment of your limiting beliefs and overactive imagination. If there's one thing I've learned over the years is that things are seldom what they first appear to be. We tend to exaggerate and stress over situations and conditions that never materialize because of the presumptive conclusions we draw. Most times we're wrong.

Once you begin eliminating limiting beliefs, your life will take on a noticeable change. You will have an almost inexplicable basis of confidence, you will be less fearful, you will begin to see (literally and figuratively) more clearly, and you will begin to understand that you can achieve anything you desire.

CHAPTER 3

Open the Vault

3 Keys to Unlock the Power of Your Mind

Our brain and our mind are two inseparably connected aspects of our psychological makeup. Our physical brain acts as the hardware that operates the psychological programs of our mind. It controls virtually every aspect of our existence—how we feel, act, learn, and function. Our mind, in turn, shapes the manner in which we define our self. The relationship between the brain (physical) and our mind (psychological) is as complex as it is awe inspiring, wondrous, and beautiful.

The brain is one of the most important and most complex of all the organs in the human body. It is made of up of a complex network of billions of cells that form the neural network which sustains life and processes information to an extent we have yet to accurately determine. The mind, operating on the functional power of the brain, allows us to process emotion, look past the obvious, create and conjure concepts, innovate, and evolve through the process of imagination and reason, which allows us to peer into the window of the metaphysical as we search for answers to *what lies ahead* and *what is it like?*

When the brain is working at peak performance it opens the pathways that allow us to be our best. We begin recognizing things that present themselves before us, *right now*. This ability opens our entire world, quite simply because we begin seeing things others cannot readily see. Ever wonder why or how some people seem to just have better luck or good fortune? The *real* secret is that they have learned to develop an ability to recognize the traits of opportunity through the power of awareness.

There are several things that influence the health and functionality of the brain and how well it develops, such as genetics, life experiences, diet and nutrition, stress, problem solving and decision-making, reading, vocabulary, and interpersonal relationships. Every one of these elements influences the brain. Despite that, however, these things do not determine or define the limits on how far we can go with respect to our personal potential.

We underestimate our power to overcome what we perceive to be insurmountable obstacles that impede, discourage, or disrupt the progress of our momentum toward personal achievement. These obstacles have the potential to cause disorder, disappointment, frustration, and disruption to our life if handled incorrectly.

So, how do we harness the power of our mind to best handle these situations? I have found the following three keys to be the most important ideas in opening the vault and unlocking the power of your mind in order to lead you to unlimited possibilities. Use these keys as a starting point to bring about the power and self-control you need to provide balance and congruence to your best life, *right now.*

⌇ Eliminate Negative Self-Talk

Our thoughts determine our feelings, beliefs, and actions. Allow that first line to truly sink in. There are so many prolific statements, quotes, and philosophies on this one aspect of unlocking the vault of our minds that we could be here all day deciphering each unique and insightful perspective. Our thoughts are so powerful that they literally dictate the direction of our life. If we believe the greatest power we have is the power of choice, then the one thing that most influences that power is the very manner we perceive the world. Our perceptions are completely driven by our thoughts. And it is our thoughts that "talk" to us, helping us navigate life, as we personally perceive it to be.

We are constantly talking to ourselves. Why, even right now—at this very moment—you are talking to yourself. We talk to ourselves at an estimated *ten times* the speed at which we speak or read. The issue, however, is not so much about the *rate* inasmuch as it is about the content or tenor of the messages we convey to ourselves.

We tend to be our own worst critics, right? Trust me—it happens even to the best of us. We walk into a room wearing our best exterior self—smile and all—while simultaneously feeding our subconscious minds with self-deprecating messages of defeat, inadequacy, and insufficiency. We tell ourselves, "I'm late…again. I'm fat. I never win. I can never find a mate. How could I be so stupid? She looks better than me. He's way more confident than I'll ever be. Must be nice to be rich." Any of these sound remotely familiar?

We constantly judge ourselves by unrealistic standards, idealistic situations, and societal definitions of what is considered acceptable or *good enough*. So whose job is it to actually set those standards anyway? If *you* are the one sending messages of self-defeat perhaps it is *you* who has assumed the role of standard bearer on what is acceptable and what is not. Wouldn't it just be better if you stopped trying to do that?

If only, then…

When it comes to negative self-talk we tend to justify our internal dialogue with what we believe is logical. We tell ourselves that we're fat, late, broke, tired, or inadequate because it is all based on what we perceive as fact. We conduct an assessment of ourselves reflecting in words what our self-talk has programmed our mind to believe. When we are fortunate enough to catch a glimpse of the alternative, we tend to reject it out of modesty or an outright refusal to believe we are good enough for the higher self-image. We justify the rejection because our perception of reality overshadows the possibility that the alternative is even possible. We tell ourselves things like, "*If only* I had a mate, *then* I'd be happier. *If only* I could wake up earlier, *then* I'd be on time. *If only* I could stick to a diet, *then* I'd be thinner. *If only* I belonged to a gym, *then* I'd be in better shape. *If only* I could win the lottery, *then* I'd be happy."

Stop living the "If only, then" life! How about this version instead…

If only you believe you are much *more* than you give yourself credit for, *then* you can be, do, or accomplish anything in life you desire…*Anything!*

74

A simple shift in your mindset is a difference-maker in terms of bringing real and lasting change to your life. It doesn't happen overnight, but it *can* happen if you'll get out of your own way and begin to focus on what's right with you instead of all the things that you've been programmed to believe are wrong. Besides, the only one telling you that there's anything wrong is...*you*.

8── Tap Into the Power of Emotional Intelligence

Chances are, you know someone who just seems to resonate very well with almost everyone they interact with, regardless of the circumstances or situation. They always seem to know what to say and how to say it. They're sometimes called chameleons—they're able to blend easily with others and are typically well-liked. They're caring and considerate, and even though they may not have solutions to fit everyone or every situation, we generally feel connected to them in such a way that we leave their company feeling hopeful, optimistic, or energized in some way. What is it that sets these people apart from the rest?

These people tend to have a high degree of emotional intelligence, often referred to as EI or EQ. They tend to know themselves extremely well, but it doesn't stop there. They are also highly receptive to the emotional needs of others. Okay, so wait just a minute. How can someone actually perceive the emotional needs of another? To explain that question, we have to first understand the basics of EQ.

According to Daniel Goleman, considered to be the authority on EQ, there are five elements that define emotional intelligence:

Self-Awareness

People with high EQ are typically very self-aware. They understand their own emotions and don't allow their feelings to cloud their judgment. As stated earlier, emotions tend to convince us of a false reality and can often lead us astray very quickly. Those with a higher self-awareness tend to trust their intuition and do a relatively good job of keeping their emotions in check.

Awareness allows us to take an honest look at ourselves from an alternative or outside perspective, which increases our ability to develop emotional intelligence. It also helps us to better recognize and acknowledge our strengths and weaknesses, effectively allowing us to continue to progress toward better performance. Many people believe self-awareness to be the cornerstone of EQ.

Self-Regulation

Our ability to control our own emotions and impulses is a crucial step in the development of EQ. People who self-regulate do not allow themselves to become over-emotional in response to external circumstances. They are not known for making compulsive or careless decisions. In other words, they think before they act. Some characteristics of a highly regulated self are thoughtfulness, integrity, sincerity, an ability to accept change, and genuine compassion for others before self.

Motivation

A distinctive personality trait of EQ is a high degree of self-motivation. Highly motivated people are willing to defer immediate results or gratification for long-term success. They are highly productive, love a challenge, possess a relentless work ethic, and love what they do. They fully understand the source of their motivation and are consciously connected to their passion and purpose. They are trusted by others, focused, and have great confidence in their own abilities. Motivated people have a passion for a challenge, readily embrace change, and love to learn and explore.

Empathy

An ability to identify and understand the desires, needs, and viewpoints of other people in social settings is perhaps the second-most important element of EQ. We define this ability as empathy. People with empathy are adept at recognizing and responding to the emotions of others, even when those feelings may not be immediately obvious. As a result, empathetic people are usually very good at managing relationships. One of the critical skills they use to accomplish this is active listening, arguably the most important life skill. Through active listening we gain critical insight on the small cues and clues offered by others that, quite often, they aren't even aware they are projecting.

Social Skills

It has been said that some people can light up a room when they arrive, or they can light it up when they leave. Which person would you rather be? For that matter, which person *are* you? Let's get real, shall we? Social skills are indeed just that—skills. In other words, they can be learned. We all recognize when someone has especially good social skills. We've spoken to them before. They are easy to talk to. Ah, there's a clue right there. Most times *we* don't even realize it when we're talking to someone with a high EQ until *after* we have left the conversation. We say things like,

"That person sure was interesting," or "She was so nice." What we probably failed to recognize was the fact that *we* were the ones doing most of the talking while *they* were actively listening. Rather than focusing on their own success, they chose instead to take an interest in yours.

What is your emotional IQ?

The good news is that EQ can be developed. If you see a need for improvement in this area, begin by observing how you react to others. Reactions are ruled by emotions. Keeping those emotions on the sidelines gives us time to process the perception of reality, removes our tendency to rush to judgment, and to use empathy instead of emotion to guide us through a casual conversation.

Self-evaluate and admit that you may have some improvements to make. Identify your weaknesses and begin working on improving them incrementally to become better. Take a critical look at how you react to stressful situations. An ability to remain calm throughout a given stressful situation accelerates your learning curve and is an invaluable trait that can go a long way in helping you to develop a higher EQ.

Although *traditional* intelligence is important to success, EQ is an absolutely essential element to relating well with others. Our ability to relate well with others is considered by some to be even more important than traditional intelligence.

⚷ Stop Resisting

In order to get the most from an open mind we must be prepared for the changes that will result. Wait a minute—

changes? Nobody told me I'd have to deal with change simply as a result of unlocking the power of my mind.

Why does the very nature of the word "change" cause so much consternation? Could it be that most people *fear* change? This question connects us with the very first key in the process of unlocking the power of our mind. Eliminating negative self-talk helps us to replace our fear of change with *anticipation* for change. You see, we have a choice when it comes to how we view change. We can fear change for what we don't know about it, or we can anticipate it for the promises it holds. Can you recognize the two distinctly different perspectives? The point is, if we have the power to choose how we look at life, why not choose the brighter alternative?

If you have reached a point in your life where you're sick and tired of the status quo, then you are in a perfect position to embrace change. If you're stuck in a perpetual cycle of getting the same results, no matter what you've tried, it may be time to finally take *action* and do something about it. Don't be consumed by what *hasn't* worked. In fact, you should celebrate knowing what hasn't worked because it serves as an indication that you're still in the game and are not about to waste any more time with unproductive efforts that yield little to no results.

One of the most exciting aspects of the concept of accepting change is that the results are immediate. Yes, *immediate!* As we change or realign our daily beliefs and behaviors, we begin to experience positive and empowering results immediately. These results are often difficult to recognize at first...unless you are *ready* to recognize them.

Half the battle in recognizing life's changes is to be in a state of true readiness and expectation. If you are in a state of readiness and expectation, your awareness is operating at peak performance and you will simply recognize things easier. By the way, it's okay to *expect* good things to come to you. Remember, however, the messages you project will return to you (very often in overwhelming abundance), so you should *expect* the return. My only caution is to be very aware of the kinds of messages you are sending, as your return will be very much the same as the messages you send forth. The old adage of "Be careful what you wish for," applies here.

All too often we believe that, in order to experience significant changes in our lives, we must implement radical behavioral and mindset changes. While radical changes may indeed result in *some* change, they typically don't yield the results we seek in terms of a lasting and positive transformation. It is the subtle changes that typically yield the best and longest lasting results. These changes come in the form of new disciplines we must be ready and willing to adopt in order to escape the bonds of our current circumstances.

The magic of new disciplines is that they cause us to *shift* our thinking in ways that transform us. Think about the new disciplines your life is calling you to make. If you truly recognize them, you will see that the changes your life is calling for you to make are not unrealistic and are often small changes (shifts) that will lead to huge differences in the results you are used to getting.

Here's a practical exercise you can do that demonstrates my point: begin with a subtle change in your posture. Instead of walking into work tomorrow in your typical tired manner, try to consciously change the position of your posture. Stand just a bit taller, lift your chin ever so slightly, smile, make eye contact, and breathe a bit deeper. You won't even have to say anything different, and people will notice. The most important aspect of this exercise is that *you* will notice. And *you* will immediately feel better about yourself. This is an *immediate* change that will empower you and compel you to seek other subtle ways in which to change the course of your life. Who knows, it could actually be the very beginning of the change you've been looking for.

Hopefully by now you can see that elevating the health of our physical body can incite a transformation to a healthier mind. Likewise, a new mindset can influence a transformation of a healthier body. Both components of the human experience influence each other in either a positive or negative manner, whichever we allow. There is also a component of an overall healthy *balanced* life that can resonate as its source or manifest as a result. That component is our *spirit*. Whatever preconceived notions you have of this word, please set them aside and pay close attention to the message, because the stool will not balance on two legs...no matter how strong they are.

SECTION THREE

Spirit

by
Kirk Hendricks

CHAPTER 1

Interconnected Being

Finding the Hidden Power of Your True Self

Spirit is a word that elicits many different reactions, depending on how we have each been conditioned to receive it. The word *spirit* has so many meanings it should be meaningless, yet it is far from it. *Spirit* maintains its individual meanings through the many connotations and associative emotions it evokes.

Consider other words with this fascinating quality. *Love* is a perfect example. *Love* has many varied meanings depending on cultural, generational, and personal perspectives. You may declare a *love* for pizza, and you may say you *love* your child. However, you don't feel the same way about a pizza as you do a child. The distinct difference between the two meanings is more than nuance, and so are the distinctions among the various meanings and connotations of the word *spirit*.

The word *spirit* could bring forth an image of a bottle of whiskey, or it may prompt the thought of an immortal soul. It may be a way of describing the essence of a person as a unique individual, or it may elicit a vision of a ghost. One is in *high*

85

spirits when they are energized and engaged, but *our* definition goes beyond these examples.

Several years before writing this book, my wife and I were talking after our children went to bed. I forget how the conversation began, but I specifically remember the details when I stated, "I feel more connected to the universe now than I have ever before." It was a feeling of wholeness, a feeling that I was part of, and not separate from, the entirety of our environment. *Spirit* is a feeling of oneness—a feeling that everything is interconnected, including you and me.

We are all interconnected within the universe through the essence of *spirit*. While the body and the mind are what we perceive as the physical, the spirit is the humbling understanding that we exist as part of a whole, the complete opposite of the conventional perspective of an isolated entity, interacting with objects distinctly different than itself. It is the *knowing of* the interconnected nature of the universe, and the accompanying feelings of honor and privilege that we get to experience our individual perspectives within that wholeness.

This part of the book will help you begin to see and nurture an understanding of *spirit*. It is additive to the previous chapters in that it completes the balance of *being*. Strong spirit, clear mind, and healthy body interact synergistically to create a sense of flow as one moves within the energy of the universe. A good first step in developing this understanding is to ask yourself a very intimate question: *Who* am I?

The answer is the beginning of a realization that there is no one there. The *self* or "the *who*" that we conventionally think of as ourselves are constructs of our mind, so a clear mind is necessary to see past these illusions. We create these ideas or concepts in an effort to make sense of our physical reality, but those very ideas distort the truth of wholeness, and hence, our *true* reality.

The untrained mind has a limited ability to understand its environment. We can allow our existence to be defined within the confines of its boundaries, or we can allow the mind to free itself from its fears and desires, paving the way to a perspective that enlivens the spirit. You may ultimately realize that you don't exist at all—no doubt a controversial statement to some—but you *will* at least come to an understanding that you don't exist in the manner your mind is naturally inclined to believe.

The uncontrolled mind constructs the mental images we have of our *self*, as well as the manifestation of the physical body we possess. The body also only exists inasmuch as our mind *thinks* it does. Our mind *thinks* it possesses a form, and this form interacts with its environment. However, our mind only *thinks* this. It is not true, so when we approach the *paradigm* from a perspective opposite the conventional view, we see the fallacy as clearly as we see the nose on our face—or *a* nose on *a* face. The mental image we have of our self and our body is an illusion arising from the untrained mind's tendency toward compartmentalization, and our *spirit*—the interconnected feeling of wholeness—is nurtured as the illusion vanishes.

We will explore the answer to *Who?* in greater detail later. Laying the groundwork for that answer begins with *What?* What is our experience of being based on? And perhaps the most important question of all, *Why?*

So, what happens when we realize we don't exist in the manner we have come to accept? Well, we begin to *see* our experiences differently. We see our interactions with the universe differently, and we see our actions, reactions, and their associated results differently. The realization that our actions do not affect something or someone else—but that they affect *us*—corrects our intent, and thus the effects of those actions, our contributions. Compassion arises, and our significance is elevated within the whole of the universe.

A subtle shift in perspective can have a major effect on our perception. We all see ourselves as fathers, mothers, daughters, sons, friends, co-workers, and many other images our mind has generated to rationalize our existence. Each mind develops its own self-image by exercising its creative power from a self-centered perspective. Our mind, therefore, is the source of who we *think* we are.

The mind is the source of all of our experiences. Its ability to sculpt each moment wields the greatest power over our life. Therefore, we must treat our mind with great care and respect as we strive to understand its limitations and allow it to free ourselves from *its* conventional reality. Careful consideration of our limitations does not come naturally, but with time, it can help us more clearly recognize the interconnected reality of our existence.

Our mind's fundamental biological objective is to keep our physical bodies alive—to keep *itself* alive. Each experience we have is a culmination of sensory stimulations we interpret and categorize to formulate a perspective from which to live and thrive. Our consciousness arises out of our body's ability to see, hear, smell, taste, and touch. Those abilities are clearly limited, so our perspective of the universe is also limited when constructed solely through our survival-based capabilities—from the inside looking out.

We can see only a very narrow band of the electromagnetic spectrum. Our ability to hear acoustic vibrations is similarly limited to a range most conducive to our survival. The same is true of our ability to taste and smell. I observe, through casual observation, that my dog and I have very different experiences on our walk. He appears to have a more complete understanding of various scents along our journey than I do, while I may have a heightened ability to contemplate our various states of awareness than he does. It is through this contemplative capability and introspective action that we are able to experience an enhanced state of being beyond our conventional animalistic reactions.

While we realize our physical body is not without limitations, we typically fail to consider how our perspective is shaped by the boundaries of our physical and intellectual capacity and to fully appreciate what lies beyond our senses. Consider that there *is* something happening within and around you at this very moment that is not an obvious part of your known experience. This "something" is an energy that exists in various states our mind cannot readily perceive. The energy is there, but it is beyond our physical ability to discern. The truth that we cannot sense every component of the universe punctuates our understanding that we don't experience reality. However, there is a reality *out there* to include what our mind knows but also encompassing the energy beyond our mind's interpretation.

Now consider the source of our experience within our environment. Every element of our conscious experience is a perceived contact with energy that is organized in a manner our physical senses recognize as *different* from ourselves. We require energy in order to exist, so the common mind instinctively creates our experiences out of that requirement and doesn't bother exploring beyond it.

The Necessity

Energy is an essential element to our survival. That truth is inherent within our mind, because our mind desires to keep the body alive. We consume nutrient-rich—and *not so* nutrient-rich—energy in order to fuel the biological processes of life. You can see this in your next meal, and with a presence of mind you can see it in your next breath.

Our mind directs our actions to absorb energy from our environment in an effort to sustain life. We require assimilation of energy into our body. In fact, our body is inextricably connected to this energy in makeup and function—energy that did not always exist in human form. We know that energy is neither created nor destroyed, so the energy we absorb to sustain life doesn't disappear, it simply changes into a form our mind can comprehend: our body.

We have the ability to realize that we are one with, not separate from, our environment. Our physical body—to include the mind—arose through an evolution and organization of the *energy of the universe*. We can physically see this, and we can intellectually understand it. However, we generally don't consider that the energy we perceive as our physical *self* to be the same energy that the entirety of the universe is made of. We tend to see ourselves as separate from the rest of the universe, but that perspective is flawed and limiting.

Consider how our physical body came into being. We consume nutrients of various forms that are used to build and promote muscle and bone growth. A tiny potential within a single living cell organizes into an adult organism out of the energy it lives within, but the physical energy we overtly identify as the human body is not the only form of energy we absorb into our concept of *self*.

Our mind is a continuous receptor and *keeper* of energy that is absorbed through its amazing capacity of transference. Every conscious moment of your life is an interactive experience with energy, and *all* of it is stored for a future recollection. For example, the image of the tree I am looking at is embedded within my mind. Anytime I wish to re-experience the moment, all I have to do is remember. This image will be with me until my mind dissolves back into the collective of the universe, along with all of the other energy it has stored. The tree may even be with me longer in some manner. *Who* knows?

The Vessel

The physical body, along with its intellectual mind, can be thought of as a warehouse of energy. We *humans*, along with all other forms, can be perceived as a vessel—a temporary repository of energy— from this perspective. That view is not demeaning. It is in fact enlightening.

We can actually visualize the interconnected nature of our *self* within the universe when we consider all of the energy we require to be *who* we are. Water within our body may have been contained in a fruit on a tree at some point in time, or it may have existed within a cloud or an ocean. When you consider the length of time this water has existed, it likely has been a component of all three. Simply stated, you—or at least a *part* of you—has existed within a fruit, a cloud, and an ocean at some point from where you currently exist.

Similarly, it is possible to understand that the carbon makeup of our body has existed elsewhere within a tree, another animal, and even as a mineral. All of the components we *think* we are made of have been flowing into and out of other objects within the entirety of the universe for a very, very long time. Now they are within us, residing among every thought our mind has ever produced.

Our thoughts—yet another aspect of energy that is used to construct the self—are generated when the energy that is our mind reacts to energy that it sees as 'not mind.' We see something like a river, and electromagnetic energy is transferred through our eyes to the visual cortex of the brain, where an image is formed. Then a thought or a judgment is generated about the image. That thought may be positive if we are hot and we believe the river can cool us, or if we are hungry and the river can feed us. *Or* that thought may be negative if the river is impeding our travels, or if it is perceived as a haven for dangerous animals. Our mind *will* place some form of judgment on the river. *That* is the mind's biological purpose: survival.

We know a river is continuously changing, never existing in the exact same manner in any two moments. However, the image of a river—good or bad—is imprinted as an object that will remain within our mind in a manner that is framed by our perceptions. The energy of each moment is captured through the lens of the mind into the medium of our emotion.

The energy of every thought we have ever had—along with its accompanying emotion—is stored within our physical body just like water. We wouldn't have any thoughts, feelings, emotions, or memories without our mind's ability to absorb the energy of the universe. We would not exist without the energy—*all* of the energy—the universe is allowing us to sculpt ourselves out of. So, you see, we simply exist as an interconnected organization of energy.

The universe has provided its elements, allowing the formation of an entity we see as ourselves, and we *get to* give back. We exist as energy interacting with energy. There is a free and active flow of energy throughout our physical body. You can visualize this energy as a stream flowing through the entity your mind defines as your *self* and back out into the continuation of the universe.

The Contribution

Every action our physical body takes is an effort to attain a goal, and every expense of energy will have future effects—*downstream* from the present. The energy we expend to take our next breath results in our continued conscious experience, and it also provides required energy for a nearby (or not so nearby) plant to continue its existence. We give the gift of a breath to the universe that allows another form to continue its journey, but as our goals become more complex, so too do the impacts of our contributions.

We require food, in addition to our next breath, to continue our own journey, and our actions in attaining it also have effects. The actions we take in providing shelter from the elements also project into the future. Now consider our actions *beyond* the necessities of survival.

The energy in a single drop of rain that rolls off a rock and into a stream effects the movement of the stream throughout its journey to the sea—even beyond. Similarly, our actions are a continuation of energy through our environment. The energy of our universe converges in and around our physical body, where we get to decide the quality of its future effects through the actions, reactions, and interactions arising from our individual and collective intent.

The contributions we make are an incredible responsibility and privilege. They are the essence of who we are—a continuation of ourselves through the end of time. However, it is a perspective that does not come intuitively to many of us. We have difficulty seeing past our most basic goal of survival, and get caught in reactive states—reactions to fears and desires.

Fear and desire are the conductors of our actions when we allow them to be. However, there is a more enlightened existence when we are able to understand our interconnected nature to everything. We have a responsibility to put *creative* effort into our actions. After all, each of us is, in some manner, a *creator* of the universe we live within.

The Creators

Our individual lives can be seen as a biological entity born into a world, interacting with it, then fading out of it—into another if you prefer. Whatever happens before birth or after death has been postulated and debated since the dawn of our ability to reason, and it will likely continue. However, we know we get to experience the middle. *Life* is, in fact, happening right now.

Many people live their life with a perspective that they are distinct and independent objects interacting among other objects—a universe of tangible *things*. However, it is possible to see our life as an organization of energy *on loan* from the universe—a temporarily organized entity receiving the gift of being. The energy of our existence is received and then given back. We exist within an energy process that simply *flows*.

The closer we look at energy as a *whole*, the more we can see from a reflective nature. This perspective provides an insightful awareness that diminishes our tendency to distinguish ourselves from everything else within our environment. It is possible—with a presence of mind—to see that the breath you inhale is the future you, while the breath you exhale is the former you, or you may simply see it as a continuation of your *self*.

A natural fear may develop when we begin to comprehend our lives as an interconnected flow of energy. This perspective gives rise to the very basic question of *who* is doing the breathing?

94

Will the future *me* of my incoming breath continue to breathe, and what will become of the former *me* of my outgoing breath? A simple shift in perspective allows us to realize that it is actually a privilege to be interconnected to every aspect of our universe.

Our *experience of being* is a creation of our mind. We can allow our mind to unskillfully produce experiences through its natural reactions to fear and desire, or we can bring clarity to our understanding and create our experiences from a truer perspective. The reactive perspective and the creative one will not change the energy you connect with, but the differences and consequences afterward, will be profound.

The feeling of unity arises when we understand ourselves as an interconnected flow of energy. Our desire to believe we are objects *separate* from the universe causes our mind to dismiss the notion that we exist within it. However, we do exist, even from a perspective of wholeness. We must *logically* exist if I am writing this and you are reading it. However, our existence is much more meaningful than the one our mind tends to generate through reactivity, so we will continue to encourage the development of spirit and its ensuing contributions. Our lives will become more fulfilling when we closely examine *who* is behind the gifts we are receiving and creating.

CHAPTER 2

Intent

Beyond Fear and Desire

The mind is the creator of the self. We can allow our mind to bring forth a self born from uncontrolled reactions, or we can harness our creative ability and understand a truer self beyond fear and desire. Understanding who we are elevates the quality of our lives and our significance to the universe—not to mention our world, society, friends, and family.

Our mind's undisciplined trickery can cloak our true significance by generating mental images of a *self* that we cling to with abandon. Our *spirit* is clouded by images, but our true nature is revealed through their dissolution. We can subdue the mind's frenzied nature and elevate our significance through the understanding and guidance of spirit.

It is important to peel back the layers and examine the core in order to understand *who* we really are, enlivening the spirit. There is a *possession* at the core, and true knowledge of that possession is the key in understanding our significance. Our spiritual nature illuminates the gifts we receive and give.

Significance

It is our nature to want our lives to have significance. We fear a meaningless life because it appears to be void, directionless, and miserable. Furthermore, we fear others will disapprove of our insignificance. We desire a rewarding life and to be the envy of others, but these desires create friction. The source of the conflict lies in our intent. Desire for significance because you don't want to appear—either to yourself or others—to be leading an empty life is an existence motivated by *fear*.

Most people are motivated by fear, and you may be no different. Do not panic. The subtle essence of your intent is the source of the quality of your significance.

Everything is revealed through the quality of one's intent, but we follow a lie that quantity is more important. We perceive a major influence on the universe as having greater significance than one that goes unnoticed, and we desire to elevate the level of our significance—our *perceived* level of significance—by generating a colossal impact.

The illusion starts with our understanding that it is more difficult to affect our families than ourselves, and is buoyed by the fact that it is more challenging to elevate a society than our families. Societies are more easily influenced than the world, and the world more so than the universe. We *think* the scope of our impact affects the significance of our life, and we fall into a trap, or a belief that we cannot be significant to the universe.

The truth is that we are all fully capable of being significant to the universe. You may not be able to immediately see it, but this book will reveal the truth as you apply logic and reason, while keeping an open mind. Quality is revealed as more important than quantity.

Our minds love to compartmentalize. Big effects are different than small ones, and we relegate significance into orders of relativity. We *believe* that doubling our income or net worth will allow us to become more significant. The economic and philanthropic effects of enormously wealthy people give credence to the *spell* of quantity.

It is important to consider a couple of points in order to bring light to relative significance. Some highly influential people were exceptionally undesirable through the quality of their intent. Take for example the impact that Adolf Hitler had on family, society, and the world and universe. You cannot argue that his impact was not significant, but nobody reading this book would desire to have that impact, to be *that* significant.

It is also important to note that some conditions are completely out of our control. Most people with excessive resources came into those resources by chance (actually, all did, but that is a philosophical topic for a different book). It is obvious that we are not in control of every aspect of the universe, but we are capable of controlling our thoughts, thus we retain full control of the quality of our intent. We get to decide our motivation, and the sincerity of our intent will determine our significance, so we must go back to the very important question of *Why?* Why do we want to be significant? Is our intent born of fear and desire, thus manifesting as reactivity, or is it rooted in love and offered through creative actions?

This is a question of enormous magnitude, because every action manifests from its intent. Answer the above question by envisioning your thoughts from the perspective of your deathbed. If you have trouble with contemplating your death, get over it. You are going to die, and that fact is *not* a problem. When you are on your deathbed reflecting on your life, what do you want to *see*, and what actions will drive you to that vision? The very thought can be quite revealing, I assure you.

Every action we take has an effect. Each will have *significance*. The significance of that action will depend on the intent it was born from. Actions motivated by fear and desire reduce the quality of your significance. Look deep inside yourself at the core of *who* you are and who you will become. Your intent is already there. Uncover your true intent, and do not be motivated by fear or desire.

The First Layers

The journey to uncover your intent starts with looking past the façade constructed by the mind. Your mind is deluded, but that's okay. *All* minds are deluded, so you are in good company. You must quiet the mind when you look within yourself. The mind does not know who you are. Your true nature is beyond your mind's delusion.

Our conventional self only exists as an image in our mind. We will call it a mind-concept image. This image is formed by intermingling all of your experiences and actions into a concept. Do something you are proud of, and your mind creates an image of a good person; or do something you are ashamed of, and your mind creates an image of a bad person. All of us have done both, and our minds twist and contort our good, bad, and insignificant actions into a concept of *self*, and it is simply a mind-concept image.

No mind is a static entity, so the mind's image of *you* moves fluidly. The images change from moment to moment, experience to experience, and journey to journey. Consider the image you had of yourself before you could ride a bike—or any other ability that comes to mind. This past image changed after you gained your new ability. In fact, this dynamic self-image continuously shifts throughout each life experience.

A different image of our self exists today than it did a year ago, and both are different than the image that existed *five* years ago. Similarly, a year ago, you had a different image of yourself than you did the year before, so our mind-concept image is like a series of images changing on the frames of celluloid film or as a series of frames on an .mvi file.

Our *mind's* image will continue to change. A different image of ourselves will exist a year from now than the one that exists at this very moment. Experiences between now and then will shape a new image generated by our mind, and one of the most beautiful truths that can be found within this book is that a new image, one within a happier and more fulfilling life, is already present at the core of who you are.

The image we create of others changes in the same manner. Consider the image you have of one of your friends. The image was different before you were friends than after. It was altered based on your experiences and interactions, but you must bring some awareness to this understanding—some *self*-awareness.

We are also an image in the minds of others. The mind-concept image of us changes through our shared experiences, and that image is different than the image we have of our *self*. We interact with hundreds or thousands of people, so there are just as many iterations of *us* interacting within the minds of others. Which image do you really think you are, and, more importantly, *what* is shaping the image of you within the minds of others? Take ownership of that *what*.

You will find truth in what is shaping the images of yourself, and understanding that truth will bring you back to your *why*. The truth of who you are cannot exist as a mind concept image, because reality does not exist in the mind. How could you possibly exist as an image of the mind when there are thousands of different images continuously changing from one form to the next?

Let's take a closer look at what our mind *thinks* is a *real* experience. Each interaction we have within our environment forms a precept influenced by our individual and unique perspective, so each experience is unique to the individual having the experience. Now consider the true nature of the experience of two people interacting with each other. There are two distinct experiences occurring within the same moment—two experiences that each individual mind *thinks* is reality. Reality becomes relative to each person. Thus, reality doesn't exist in our mind. Our mind creates *its* own reality through the images it interprets, and these illusory images cloud our true nature.

Our *own* reality happens *within* us. It does not happen *to* us. Our mind shapes our experiences and forms the image we have of the *self*. The self is not a creation of birth, education, work, play, tragedy, or success. The self is a creation of the mind. You are the creator of yourself, and all creative action flows from a source. The source from which we create our self doesn't lie at the surface. It takes discipline and creativity to uncover, and that journey requires dissolution of the layers our untrained mind forms through its self-*ish* motivation.

A Closer Look

Now, who do we really think we are? Really, *who* do we think we are? There must logically be some *thing* in order for us to have significance, so what is the nature of the object we *think* of as our self? This is one of the most important questions we can ask, and the answer—if we are honest—is a humbling gift to be treasured. This book is intended to provide some perspectives that will help uncover the answer.

When asked who I am, I typically respond with, "Kirk Hendricks." But this is not *who* I am. My name is a series of words—one word that someone labeled me with, followed by another word I inherited. I would not be someone different if I used different words, so the words cannot be *who* I am.

You most likely know your parents' names and your grandparents' names. It is less likely you know your great-grandparents' names and still less likely you know your great-great-grandparents' names. You don't have to go very far back to understand that the words by which we are labeled are insignificant. The people, however, were *very* significant. That is, they made a significant contribution to the universe. A label is simply an insignificant, distracting sound.

Unskillful actions motivated by fear or desire construct a self through labels of images, and the source of those actions maintains the illusion. My mind naturally reacts poorly when I say, "I am not Kirk Hendricks." Try it for yourself, using your own name. You see, there is a natural fear of not knowing. These words just don't sit well with the self we have *let* our mind generate. It takes courage and perseverance to continue through these layers, but I assure you, understanding and bringing creative action through the *source* is worth it.

Once we understand that we are not just a series of syllables that form words, we begin using concepts like relationships (family or otherwise), careers, hobbies, physical locations, and in the worst case, possessions, but none of these can ultimately answer who we are. These concepts are simply more images the mind has assigned labels to. We must not fool ourselves into thinking we are a conglomeration of concepts and things. We still have significance when the *things* are removed.

Many people I know would say their soul is who they are, but let's approach the question with logic and reason. The concept of a soul is a creation—like all *things*—of the mind, and if each mind creates its own reality, then there are countless concepts and ensuing images of the soul. Do not allow your mind to create a self that is based on *any* labeled images. We will not discount metaphysical beliefs on our journey, but we will maintain logic and reason. And we will do so without fear or desire.

Let's move through the next layers. Our experiences provide some compelling images. Some people believe they are a mold filled with their individual life experiences, and their mind contemplates consciousness of these experiences as the *self*, which leads to the obvious question of what consciousness actually is. The cutting edge of science does not yet have a model, and its eventual understanding will still not contain the answer. However, we *are* onto something as we consider our experiences.

Every experience we have is an interaction between our mind and its contact with energy; energy that it sees as separate from itself. We contact energy through our senses, and that contact is sent to our brain where the mind generates a precept—a judgment about the energy. This is the foundation of the concept we *believe* is our separate self.

The energy we contact is necessarily organized differently than our own bodies in order for there to be contact. Thus, we are presented with two separate objects—the object of our contact and the object of our self. Next, the mind creates an experience out of the contact. A phenomenon is occurring, and if something is happening, it must be happening to some-*thing*. The concept of self is born, because an experience cannot take place without someone to experience it. *You* become the experiencer.

Your mind *infers* you exist as the experiencer, but this process contains a conundrum. The experience cannot happen without the subject (you) to experience it, *and* it cannot happen without an object (the universe) to experience. The experiencer and experienced—subject and object—require each other. They are inseparable. You are the energy of your experience, *and* the energy of your experience is you.

It may take some time to realize the universe is you and you are the universe, but we will get there together. After all, *we* are one. Our minds separate us through a clever use of images, but the images dissolve the more closely we examine them.

The *self* our mind conventionally creates is an illusion. Thus, the *self* our mind has created cannot be significant, but we bring significance to ourselves and the universe through the quality of our actions and, more importantly, the quality of our intent. Whatever we *think* is indeed the reality we create for our self—a *self* that will become increasingly significant through understanding and acceptance.

Now we are getting to the core of who we *really* are, beyond the labels, concepts, and images. We can possess or be possessed by the *self*. The difference is simply a matter of awareness. We *get to* allow the manner in which we receive, experience, and give back the gift that is our *self*. Tear down the walls, peel back the layers, and see for yourself the elegant simplicity of being.

CHAPTER 3

Possession

Affecting Our Contribution

You *think* you actually own things. Don't deny it. Everyone does. The problem is, you only *think* this or, rather, your *mind* thinks this. Your mind is telling you that you possess things, but this cannot be. You haven't even figured out *who* you are yet, so how could *you* possibly own anything? In reality, there is no *you* to be the owner, and there are no *things* to be owned. It would be more appropriate to say that the things in your mind actually possess *you*—whoever that is.

Our most precious possessions are not even ours. Every*thing* is an illusion, even our mind and our body. Don't worry. You do have at least one *real* possession. It arises within you, and it will last forever. When you see it, you will understand how you, too, will last forever.

Ownership

My dog thinks he has possessions, much the same as we humans do. He thinks he owns a soccer ball—several, actually—and he thinks he owns a branch I cut off a tree. He even thinks he owns my socks when he is fortunate to come across an unguarded pair. However, he—along with every one of us—is delusional. His mind is molding a *reality*, and he has fallen under its spell. My dog does not own things, and neither do we. However, we have the creative capacity to see past the façade of our *mind's* reality.

In order to unveil the truth, we have to start by asking our self what this concept of ownership really means. What is ownership, and what could we possibly ever *really* own? The answer is the next step on the path to understanding *who* we really are. Follow closely because that understanding will directly impact the rest of your life and its significance.

Ownership and possession are one and the same. One cannot exist without the other—they only exist as relative concepts in our mind. Objects and possessions are thoughts, *not* reality.

When we scrutinize these concepts more closely, there are a couple of ideas that we generally accept without question. Ownership and possessions necessarily require an owner and an object, so let's exercise our mind beyond blind acceptance. Some important questions arise as we explore beyond the ordinary. After all, isn't that why you are reading this book—to answer questions and to realize an extraordinary existence?

First, consider *your* concept of an owner. The owner—*you*—doesn't really exist; at least the owner doesn't exist in the manner the mind conventionally thinks it does. Please go back to the last chapter if you are still having trouble with this. We need to see past the mirage that our minds have created for us in order to find the real self. We *must* see beyond our mind.

Second, we need to examine the true nature of the *possession*—the things we think we own. Our mind creates a world of things because it is trying to keep our physical bodies alive, and that is okay. However, objects of ownership are not real. Our home, car, boat, or jet airplane don't really exist. *Our* own existence is more real than the things we think we own, and we are getting closer to the true nature of that existence. For now, we should understand that the *things* our mind thinks it owns don't really exist, and we can prove it through logic and reason, along with an open mind.

Tangible Things

What did you own when you came into this world, and what will you own when you leave? The common answer is *nothing*, but that answer is uninspiring, so...prepare to be inspired.

Let's view these objects of ownership from the perspective of their *energy streams* to help dissolve the mind's delusion. Every*thing* can be seen from an energy perspective. Everything arises from a source of energy, seemingly creating an object, and eventually everything dissolves back into energy, which we have come to embrace as *the universe*. We know—or at least we *say* we know—that nothing lasts forever. However, we don't generally portray an inarguable realization of that understanding. In other words, we tend *not* to see that *nothing* is the same—*exactly* the same—from one moment to next. Your mind, encumbered by its limitations, is incapable of perceiving many of these changes, so it *thinks* some things exist and *knows* other things do not. It is, in fact, creating conflict within itself.

For example, we think of a river as a body of water forever imprinted within the contours of the landscape, even though we can see that it is constantly changing. It *exists* as something different from one moment to the next. That is, it exists inasmuch as our mind creates a concept of an object, and so does everything else.

I'm reminded of a conversation I had with a friend over twenty years prior to the publication of this book. It was a conversation about—you guessed it—possessions. He thought he owned his home, but fortunately for him, I was there to show him otherwise. His was a nice house on a small private lake where he could canoe and fish whenever he desired. His house was nicer than mine, and he didn't react well when I suggested that he didn't *really* own it.

"It's *my* house," he stated.

"What makes it yours?" I replied.

"I have a deed that says it's mine."

A government organization gave my friend a piece of paper that said he owned his house, so his mind *thought* he owned it. My friend and the government—also a mind concept image—were caught in the delusion that an object that didn't *really* exist could be owned by a person who hadn't *really* figured out who he was, *yet*.

"Let's talk about what your house is made of," I said, as I considered my position of logic and reason. "Your house is mostly made of lumber, right?"

"Yes," my friend responded hesitantly.

"So, where did this lumber come from?" I asked.

My friend replied with the obvious answer: "Trees."

"You own trees?" I probed further.

"No," he replied. "They are not trees anymore. Now they are lumber."

There it was!

The trees *turned* into lumber, and lumber only existed as former trees. They could not exist as anything else. There must be trees in order for there to be lumber, inasmuch as lumber exists as a concept in our mind, in a name. Energy flows from a tree form to a lumber form, but it doesn't start with trees.

Consider what must exist before there are trees. Seeds, water, sunlight, and carbon dioxide—for the most part—must be present. Trees require these materials to come together, and lumber requires the processing of trees, so lumber requires water, light, and so on. My friend's house required lumber, so he actually owned former sunlight. Get it? You can go back indefinitely to the beginning of the universe, if you choose.

You can also go forward. What will his house look like in fifty years, or one thousand? You know it won't last forever, so eventually it will dissolve back into the universe only to appear as a different *thing* in the future. Everything our mind conceives as an object of experience can be seen from this perspective—from the perspective of an energy stream—and the energy stream is continuously flowing just like the river.

The energy your mind thinks of as an object has always existed in some other form or fashion. Similarly, the thing—or at least the energy that it currently consists of—will continue to exist until the end of time. The energy flows like a stream, and it continuously changes from one moment to the next, so how can we be so arrogant as to think we own any part of the energy of the universe? We don't. Our mind only *thinks* we do.

Consider any single object, the cup you are drinking from or this book you are reading. Ask yourself how it came to be, what it is, and what it will look like when it ceases to be. Furthermore, consider how everything changes from moment to moment. Everything you can imagine is made of energy that looked different than it does in this moment. You may be able to see the changes, like a constantly moving river, and you may not, like the slowly rotting timbers in your house. Make no mistake though—everything *is* changing. Everything is *flowing*.

Our mind has a way of capturing moments. Like a camera, the mind captures and reflects you as a mind-concept image. When you see past yourself from this perspective you can see you are constantly changing from moment to moment. Everything else also exists in this fluid state, and when something is changing or flowing slower than our mind can perceive, our mind captures an image and gives it a name. However, it is nothing more than a mind concept image, a snapshot in a moment of flowing energy.

Every experience we have can be ultimately viewed as energy interacting with energy. Anything that exists outside of this intermingling flow would be outside of the scope of our perception. Our senses—also made of organized energy— inherently require contact with other forms or sources of energy to create an experience.

Let's examine the chain reaction of our mind's misunderstanding of reality. Our mind believes something exists as it is initially presented, especially if the object has a perceived value. Our mind then convinces *itself* that we (ourselves constantly changing concepts) have ownership of an object (another constantly changing concept). Can you see that neither our mind nor we can really *own* anything? Can you see past that? If you cannot, then your mind owns you. Your mind's possessions own you, and you, yourself, are possessed. Hopefully *that* got your attention, but there is still one more delusion to see past, something personal.

Your physical body is also made of the same energy as every other *thing*. Energy enters your body, and energy leaves your body. The energy doesn't change, it flows. Physicists know this as the law of conservation of energy. Energy can neither be created nor destroyed. There is a profound wisdom found in the perspective of this law, especially considering that no *thing* lasts forever—including your body—so, as we have clearly discovered, you don't *really* own that either.

Your Body?

I just caught you off guard. Admit it. Even if you were following me intuitively on how *things* are merely concepts of our minds, when I suggest that you don't own your body that may be a bit disconcerting. That's because our own body is such a personal possession, and instinctively, our mind reacts.

You still cannot see who you really are *if* you believe you own your body. The question was posed earlier about what you owned when you came into this world, and that question is answered for you—*nothing*. However, most may have assumed the focus was on external things in our environment, things our minds fear, or desire. The physical image of our body most likely did not occur as one of these things, because there is something so personal about that *thing* that our mind doesn't even question it. However, *everything* should be questioned.

Our mind doesn't question whether we own our body, because our mind is part of the physical makeup of the body. The mind's job is to keep the body alive, and if you have not yet acknowledged that you are more than a mind-concept image, then you still *think* you own your body. That's okay. Most people do. But to find out *who* we really are, we must look past that mistaken perspective.

Our body isn't a *thing* to be owned—nothing is—so how could we own it? Our body is no different than any other object when you understand how it is formed and how it will disintegrate.

In fact, our mind can see that our body is constantly changing more overtly than something inanimate such as our home, but it tells us that we possess it. Our mind, in reality, possesses us. We cannot own a river, and we do not own our body. However, the energy that is your body is currently on loan from the totality of the universe, so you do have an obligation to care for it.

Your mind wants to make this personal, so let's get personal. Consider the last sip of water you drank—by the way, you should drink more water. We need to ask some questions about this water. It may have been contained in a bottle you purchased, or it may have come from a faucet in your kitchen. Either way, you probably *thought* you owned it, or at least your mind framed it that way. The water—made of energy flowing freely throughout the environment—moved from outside your body to the inside. Do you still own it?

You answered yes, unless you have noticed the pattern—unless you are beginning to see the *who* that you are. We think we own our bodies, so the water—which is now part of our body—is ours, even though we may not be sure who *that* is. So, how do we see things after the water leaves our body? Do we still own it? You may think not, but if you owned it before it entered your body and also while it was *in* your body, then you own it after it leaves, don't you? If so, *you* are a litterbug.

You are not a litterbug, because you never actually *owned* the water. Now consider every other form of energy that passes through your body. Do you think you own it? You *don't*, so why do you think you do? Why do you *think* you own the physical form of your body?

It all comes back to our mind's sense of self. Our mind cannot get over it, and it makes a convincing case to us. However, we need to see *who* we are beyond our mind's limited attempt to make sense of our existence. Yes, we do exist, and the *self*—the *who*—beyond our mind's uninspiring concept-image is an amazing and incredible entity that will continue on until the end of time.

I hope you can see past your mind's attempt to separate yourself from the totality of the universe. It is necessary to destroy that illusion if you are to ever find your true value. Your value lies in the energy that flows through you and into the future. *Our* value exists within our *action*.

Action

Every action you take is an expenditure of energy toward an end. That is, there is a goal to be attained. The most basic goal (to take another breath) and the most profound (*self*-discovery) are both attained through our action. Remember that, because *action* is the only path to goal attainment.

We experience energy, and there is energy in action. Our actions determine how we move towards our goals, and we will discover who we are in that journey. Action is the vehicle that allows us to give the gift of our significance back to our family, friends, society, the world, and universe. *Now* things are getting interesting. We are getting to the *who* and to an understanding of our *only* possession.

Everything is the result of a cause. The lumber in your house resulted in the cause of someone processing a tree into some*thing* else. The tree was the result of other causes including water—which you may have once thought you owned.

What is the difference between the tree and the house? *You* are the difference. Your actions determine what the tree becomes. Your actions result in effects. *That* is what you own, and the effects of your actions will echo eternally. Yes, your only possession is the only thing that lasts forever.

Every thought and movement is the beginning of a chain of reactions. Some call this karma. I call it logic and reason, and we will maintain logic and reason—along with an open mind—as we discover who we are. Every goal invokes action, and every action has consequences or effects.

The effects of a stone dropped into a pond will ripple waves of energy outward from its source of impact. The same is true of the effects of your actions toward your goals. The resulting ripples of energy will not stop. You move energy with your actions, and that energy will continue to move in the direction of your intent, influencing everything in comes into contact with.

Hate flows across our field of reality like ripples on water and affects everything it contacts. Fortunately, so does love, and even *more* fortunately, we *get to* decide. We get to decide what our goals are and what actions we take. That is who we are, and that is our only possession. The effects of our actions continue beyond our conventional lives and our spirit also continues, living within them.

Intent

Intent is our only possession, and what else could we ask for? We get to determine the quality of our contributions. We own the source of the ripples we send across the universe, the source of our immortality. That fact becomes clear when we see past the *reality* our mind attempts to create for us.

You are your intent, and your intent is you. This realization is a gift that liberates the possessed spirit, the spirit possessed

114

by things. Remember the things? How trivial they seem now, at least in light of our only true possession—an eternal gift.

Those of us who think we own things are not the possessors. We are the possessed. We *see* things we love and other things we despise. *Fear* of the things we despise and *desire* for the things we love possess our thoughts, and they direct our (possessed) actions. It is time to take ownership of your true *self* and your actions.

You are the creator. That is the essence of everything. You *get* to create your only possession—your intent—and your intent manifests in the reflection of a true reality. The gift of the reality you create is everlasting. The results of your actions are immortal, and within them, so are you. The (very big) question is how will you choose who you *get* to be? Choose wisely, because whatever you create *will* indeed last forever.

Take Action Today!

B alance is *the* essential state to a happy and fulfilling life. Without it, our life is devoid of the experiences we require to function effectively and with any degree of happiness and harmony. Just as sleep is an essential aspect of our ability to function physically and emotionally, so too is the need for equilibrium across the three aspects of our existence.

The manner in which we construct our life has a lot to do with whether or not we find and experience balance to any degree of consistency. In other words, our *choices* have a lot to do with the condition or circumstances we define as our specific quality of *life*. The fact that choices or decisions play such a pivotal role leaves little doubt that we can all *take action* to realign our lives to a state that reflects, in fact ensures, a more consistent life balance.

Consider the changes that have taken place over our very own lifetime that reflect man's attempt to find balance, yet our quest to do so has only further led to the frustrations that shroud the very thing we seek.

"We have bigger houses but smaller families; more conveniences but less time. We have more degrees, but less sense; more knowledge, but less judgment; more

experts, but less solutions; more medicine, but less healthiness. We've been all the way to the moon and back, but have trouble crossing the street to meet a new neighbor. We have built more computers to hold more information, to produce more copies than ever, but communicate less. We have become long on quantity but short on quality. These times produce tall men with short character; steep profits but shallow relationships. It is a time when there is much in the window but nothing in the room."

~ **Dalai Lama**

It is increasingly clear that, in order to find balance, we must make concerted efforts to overcome the distractions and disillusions that often prevent us from discovering the true source of frustrations we occasionally have with life. The wisdom behind *333 The Power of Equilibrium* goes a long way in bringing about the resolutions we seek as we endeavor to gain insight to areas we find deficient. Discovering these areas is but a first step in the process of addressing equilibrium. We must also follow through by taking *action* to make the necessary adjustments that are required to produce the very balance we seek. Doing so changes the entirety of how we see the world and ultimately brings a new level of quality to our experience of life.

What aspect of your life is out of balance? What can you do to realign things to a state of equilibrium that will bring you closer to the kind of life you truly desire and ultimately deserve? Consider the perspectives brought forth in this book as a beginning to your own personal journey of discovery and to a quality of life that brings real happiness to the forefront of everything.

Body

Our physical body is the *only* vessel we have to experience the full nature of life. Like it or not, we are charged with the responsibility to keep it in optimal working order for as long as we care to enjoy the experiences of life. We *get to* decide how well it functions by the decisions we make to (literally) care and feed it—the consequences of which either reward us richly or punish us unapologetically. Consider the pivotal role your physical body plays in the quality of *your* life. Go back and review the words and wisdom of author Colleen Riddle to discover the details you may have missed the first time. Challenge yourself to make *one* change that will add to the quality of your life through physical activity and better nutrition. Take *action* by making a conscious decision to turn away from foods that rob you of the quality of life you deserve. Conduct an honest assessment of your own physical condition, and make a conscious choice to dig deep to discover *why* you should make a choice to change *right now*. You already know whether or not this applies to you to any degree, so…what are you waiting for?

Mind

Your perception of life was formed by the *perspective* of your experiences. By reading this book you have pushed your mind to look beyond the limitations of your ability to interpret life experiences. You have learned how to step away from yourself in such a way as to begin to look at life from a selfless point of view. Doing so has allowed you to increase your perspective through the aspect of awareness, insight, and introspect. Our mind serves a crucial role in the combined effect of the interactive harmonious balance with the physical and spiritual aspects of the self. To ensure our psychological and emotional balance we must feed and care for our mind in much the same way we care for our physical body. This takes a conscious effort that begins with our choice to fortify this area of the triad. In other words, for change to occur, we must *act*. Take action *right now* by making incremental changes that bring about a new level of awareness to the forefront of your life. Allow the words and insight of author Gary Westfal to resonate as you remember to stand taller, look people in the eye, and recognize the sights, sounds, and scents that have always been a part of the human experience. Begin at once to acknowledge these things as you go about your day, and watch the *Power of Equilibrium* play out in a very profound way.

Spirit

There is a connection to everything that goes beyond our ability to fully appreciate the nature of the human role in life. We do the best we can to define our *true self* through the limitations of our capacity to define the often elusive nature of the human spirit. We see "empty space" between our physical selves and other tangible objects, and elements of life through the limited reasoning we have. We conclude that everything is unique and separate, when, in fact, it is completely the opposite. As author Kirk Hendricks eloquently surmises, it is time to take ownership of your true self through *action*. He adeptly reminds us that we are the creators of our intent, which essentially defines our reflection and understanding of a true reality. It is a spiritual concept that transcends religion or opinion. Consideration of this perspective is one in which the truth will reveal itself through a personal resonance that better enables you to manage this aspect of life to bring balance to the fore. Your spiritual self is an aspect of life in which you can indeed take action to better understand...if it is truly your *intent* to do so.

ABOUT THE AUTHORS

Gary Westfal burst onto the writing stage when his first critically acclaimed novel, *Dream Operative*, achieved an Amazon #1 ranking in the thriller genre in its first year of publication—a phenomenal feat for a first-time novelist. His writing has been consistently compared to seasoned thriller writers like Brad Thor, Tom Clancy, Vince Flynn, and Joseph Finder. Gary developed his passion for writing purely by coincidence. A frequent and lucid dreamer, Gary began documenting his dreams on paper in order to better understand the alter-conscious phenomenon and his self on a deeper level. What began as an exercise in self-prescribed therapy through documentation, turned out to be much more than he expected, and eventually led to the creation and publication of his first novel.

Gary publishes his work under his own label, the G-Life Enterprises Corporation (https://glifeenterprises.com). He personally creates the concepts for his cover and jacket designs using the artistic talents of some of the best graphic artists in the industry. As a speaker and personal coach/mentor, his inspiring personality and charisma are contagious attributes, whether in casual, one-on-one conversation or speaking to large audiences. His lecture and presentation skills can best be described as confident, engaging, and articulate.

He is the creator and chief contributor to *Introspection* (http://gwestfal.blogspot.com/), a periodic blog that provides thought-provoking topics seeking to enrich the lives of his readers by challenging them to think deeper, look within themselves for answers, and to be mindful of the value of the present moment. The blog offers a fresh perspective on personal empowerment and a wide range of human interest topics while providing a canvas of thoughts and introspect leading to a better understanding of the elements that are connected to true happiness, balance, and harmony in life. He frequently speaks to audiences about human motivation, inspirational narratives, and practical business applications.

Colleen Riddle is a full-time entrepreneur and health and fitness expert living in paradise. She grew up as a competitive swimmer and learned early on how good it felt to set goals, work hard, and win. Having these skills helped her to achieve her ultimate childhood goal of receiving a swimming scholarship to Florida State University. Go Noles!

As the owner of Elite Physique Personal Training, Colleen's passion for fitness and expertise in nutrition is evidenced by her contagious positive personality and her ability to connect tangible results to the needs of her clients. From losing weight to creating an overall healthy lifestyle, improving skills as a competitive athlete, or creating a new fitness mindset, the results she consistently achieves are matched only by the absolute best in the business.

Colleen's DVD Series, *New Mommy Makeover,* is a brilliant series inspired by the passion she has for life beyond the joy of child bearing. The series received rave reviews in *Fit Pregnancy* magazine and was voted the Number One Post Natal DVD fitness series and is a must have for new moms.

As a monthly contributor to *Destin Life Magazine* and a featured fitness entrepreneur in *Inc. Magazine*, her insightful articles convey the passionate message she has about the overall wellness of others. From proper exercise mechanics to creating the right mindset for consistent results, the wisdom and practical knowledge she offers is delivered in a spirited and delightful manner that resonates across her wide readership demographics.

For fun, Colleen enjoys spending time outdoors along the beautiful beaches of northwest Florida. She has been married to her wonderful husband and best friend, John for twenty years. They have two hilarious cats—Starsky and Hutch—that keep them entertained on a regular basis.

Colleen has been an entrepreneur for over seventeen years. She loves the freedom as well as the challenges that come with the journey. She is passionate about empowering others to see their own true greatness while creating the lifestyle they've always wanted. *333* is her first book.

Kirk Hendricks enthusiastically writes about perspective shifts intended to help people lead happier and more fulfilling lives. His book, *The Sunset's Present*, is a guide to help people realize the intangible but deeply meaningful interconnectivity they already possess within their environment and how to approach life from a perspective of wholeness. Kirk frequently speaks to groups on topics of personal empowerment and the importance of properly setting and attaining goals.

Raised in the rural Midwest, Kirk enjoys a small town lifestyle, currently residing on Florida's Gulf Coast. He sees every opportunity as a chance to enjoy a new experience, from the nuances of a day at the beach with his family to the exhilaration of traveling to new and exciting destinations. Kirk is a deep thinker whose perspectives offer refreshing insight and a bit of challenge to traditional paradigms. His comfortable, warm, and charming nature invite intrigue and sets the tone for deep, meaningful and non-judgmental discussions worthy of consideration beyond the customary bounds of what is thought to be spiritually possible and plausible. The white sandy beach of his adopted home is the perfect backdrop from which his own spirit has discovered the peaceful nature from which to ride upon the waves of insight he has gained over the years.

Kirk earned his Bachelor of Arts and Masters of Science in degrees in biology and is a leadership professional with over twenty years of experience in sales and marketing. He enjoys family activities, cooking, food and wine pairing, and exercising outdoors. His most fulfilling duties are as a husband and father of two girls.

Your reviews and recommendations are vital to the success of every author.

If you enjoyed reading this book, please help by leaving a positive review on Amazon and other social media sites and by recommending this book to others.